HOLY GROUND

STELLA JACOBS

BALBOA
PRESS
A DIVISION OF HAY HOUSE

Balboa Press books may be ordered through booksellers or by contacting:

Balboa Press
A Division of Hay House
1663 Liberty Drive
Bloomington, IN 47403
www.balboapress.com
1 (877) 407-4847

Print information available on the last page.

ISBN: 978-1-5043-9772-8 (sc)
ISBN: 978-1-5043-9774-2 (hc)
ISBN: 978-1-5043-9773-5 (e)

Library of Congress Control Number: 2018902745

Balboa Press rev. date: 08/17/2018

Dedication

To my three children, my cherubs
I wouldn't want to take the journey with anyone other than the three of you. I hope you see resilience in response to my mistakes, showing that rising again is more important than what or who took you down.

To my beloved dogs, who know all my secrets
You never left my side through it all. Those days you rested your heads gently on my shoulder did not go unnoticed. The hikes we've shared and the love you have shown will live in my heart forever.

To my mother
Throughout my life, you have shown me, by example, how to march forward with resilience, pride, and purpose.

Acknowledgments

To my therapist, Sharyn, from the bottom of my heart, thank you for guiding me through this harrowing pilgrimage. You helped me to face fear, to laugh, and to love myself again; you brought me back to life one vertebra at a time.

To my designer, Deborah Perdue, for my book cover and layout, words cannot express my gratitude for your professional excellence. Thank you for offering referrals and for bringing this book to fruition. You led the charge in creating an editing team that promoted unified collaboration and vision. Just when I thought this project would never be finished, I found you.

To my editor, Joni Wilson, your expert editing has polished my story in ways that I could not. You have taught me so much, helping me to hone my writing craft far beyond my expectations. I hired an editor and discovered a colleague.

To my talented illustrator, Tara Thelen, the book cover artwork you created is a perfect match to what I envisioned. Thank you for your artistic talent and participation.

To my readers, thank you for walking this narrative path alongside me. Don't ever give away your strength, for it is yours to keep forever. You are wise. You are worthy. Love yourself always.

Hollow Ground is a chronicle of events to show others in parallel situations that you can free yourself from domestic abuse and move on to live with the ease you desire. I did not fully comprehend the toxic existence in which I lived until I found my voice. I hope my story helps you to find yours.

Contents

Introduction

I LIVED A CLICHÉD LIFESTYLE in the upscale, suburban town of Larington, Massachusetts—until one day I met a stranger who would change my life forever.

Realizing too late that he was not the man he presented himself to be, I struggled to recapture my strength and dignity, as I strategized my exit from the psychopathic man I had once trusted and loved.

At a crossroad, I am left with two questions: If I could break away from my abuser, not knowing the consequences or the outcome of that choice, would I do it? If I had the chance to transport myself to a permanent shift in my life, would I take that path?

Chapter 1

Larington, Massachusetts, March 2, 2011

NEW ENGLAND BREEDS STRONG, hearty people who pride themselves on their winding roads; crisp, clean air; and the ever-changing hues of the seasonal landscape. Winter weather seldom stops them. Today is one of those rare days when it does.

This morning, Larington has officially shut down as the snowplows that began at 2:00 a.m. do their best to keep ahead of the storm that has dropped over 18 inches of snow overnight. There are few options on days like this, other than to relinquish control by snuggling under the covers and settling in to the serenity of a snow day.

Propped up by pillows and a hot tea on my bedside, I channel-surf while petting my dog, Riley. His head is burrowed into the blankets, his body keeping me warm as he snores softly. The household is in a winter slumber, as the wind howls and the snow continues to pack itself against the house, creating an acoustic density on the inside. I like the cozy effect.

The local meteorologist on the TV, dressed in snow-day attire of a winter sweater instead of the standard suit and tie, announces that schools are canceled for today. I can hear my two daughters, Julia and Zoey, cheering from their beds after learning they can now sleep the morning away. The gift of a snow day is one of the perks of a north-eastern childhood.

My daughter Julia, a high-school sophomore, will lounge the day away. A welcome break from her hectic schedule of academics and athletics practice. Zoey, my middle-school daughter, will soon wake, because she likes to celebrate snow days with a hearty breakfast of pancakes and bacon. Harris, my eldest and a college freshman, is comfortably settled in Arizona, far away from the snow drifts that cling to the windows.

Julia soon enters the bedroom with her usual flair. Wrapped in a towel with dripping wet hair, she stands directly in front of the TV, breaking the dazed solitude I have been lost in. Her hands rest authoritatively on her hips. Her stance insinuates that she expects me to read her mind.

"What?" I ask from the warmth of my bed.

"Notice anything out of the ordinary?" Julia asks.

"Why, yes," I say. "That's a lovely hairstyle you've chosen for today."

"Not even funny, Mom. Why don't we have hot water?"

"What? What do you mean, we don't have hot water!" Swinging my legs out of bed, I bolt to the nearest sink and then to each sink in the house, turning on faucets and wishing the water to become warm to the touch—but all I feel is cold.

"No! Not today!" I grumble. "I'll never get anyone out here with this snow!

Damn it!" I say quietly, as I realize there will be no leisurely hot shower for any of us today. I was told months ago that my water heater was on its last legs. Having ignored that warning is going to make for a complicated day.

Chapter 2
March 3, 2011

THE NEXT DAY AT 11:00 a.m., on the morning of what would have been my father's eighty-first birthday, my doorbell rings. It's been eight years since he passed away. It doesn't seem possible. As I walk toward my front door, I feel a transfer of energy, a presence telling me to pay attention. It's not the first time I've received subliminal messages like this. They come to me every so often, and now I wonder what today's message might contain. I feel a surge of energy pass through my body as I pause with my hand on the doorknob; I feel nervous and excited at the same time.

Pay attention? For what? I ask myself. I answer the door. I meet the eyes of the man standing there, and we fixate on each other, holding an unexpected gaze a few seconds longer than usual. At this moment in time, my life blooms into vibrant, beautiful colors, not knowing that soon, the sturdy earth beneath me will slowly turn to hollow ground.

Reaching out to shake my hand, he says with a smile, "Hi. My name is Jake. I spoke to you yesterday about your water heater."

"Yes, please come in."

He steps through the front door, trying to brush the snow from his boots, while I carefully scan him up and down as we make our way to the basement. He has a presence about him.

At 6 feet tall, he is ruggedly handsome. His broad shoulders grab my attention, while he makes jokes and lies on the floor to examine the damage. He rolls over onto his back and pushes himself to stand, towering over me in height as he states the inevitable. I need a new water heater, but he has rigged the old one to work temporarily.

"Go easy on the hot water until I come back with a new one in a few days." Our conversation has just a hint of sugar mixed in as his blue eyes speak directly to mine. I'm not a serial dater, and I'm known to be shy in these circumstances, but this time I'm slightly on edge from the instantaneous attraction taking place between us.

As he writes up a quote, he leans in close to me. "Who makes the decisions in the house?"

I answer, "Me." I know it's the answer he wants to hear.

I hold my breath as I watch him, feeling pleasantly nervous and flattered with the attention. We chat casually, both of us aware of the mutual attraction, as we linger a bit longer than necessary.

Now finished with the service call, I reach out to shake his hand, hoping that, if I glance just a moment longer into his eyes, he'll know I'm interested. It's a bold move for me, given my bashful ways.

I've been through divorce, the highs of falling in love and the lows of leaving it behind. But one can always hope there is someone out there who is the missing piece to one's lifelong puzzle. Could it be possible that I met a special guy on my father's birthday? I think back to the surge of energy I received just moments before opening my door to this man. *Pay attention?*

While I am not able to decipher the meaning, I know it pertains to this attractive guy I just met. Should I move forward or turn away? I see these subliminal messages as a blessing and a curse, but quite honestly, I'm stumped this time. One thing I do know is that I would like to see this man again.

Once he leaves, I call my mother's phone and quietly say to her, "I'm not sure what just happened, but I think I might have met someone special."

A week passes, and my mind is still lingering on this new man. The curiosity is getting the better of me, as I wonder if the flirtation we shared has the potential to lead anywhere.

After all the anticipation of the new water heater, I am disappointed when I have to postpone the installation for a week, leaving me to wonder whether the spark shared between us would fade with the delay. With our first meeting still weighing pleasantly on my mind, I chalk it up to a simple flirtation going nowhere. I figure he's probably in a relationship anyway; our initial introduction is getting stale by this point.

The evening after I postpone the installation, my cell phone buzzes with a text message from Jake. "Sorry you had to reschedule. I can fix your water heater anytime you're ready." Before I can respond, he sends a second text: "I work for wine. LOL."

A tad confused, I wonder whether this is a business flirtation—*or is he asking for a date?* I respond strategically so I can explore the possibilities, starting off with a low-key suggestion of 5:00 p.m. on Wednesday at a local wine bar. A safe proposition to start. It's not too assertive yet not too dismissive.

He declines my offer with a far better suggestion. "How about Sunday afternoon in the North End?" I am smiling from ear to ear. My face is flushed. *Bingo on the flirtation*, I think.

Without knowing anything about me, Jake has managed to pick my favorite spot in Boston for our first date, the neighborhood where I lived during my college years. This sparks my interest in him even further. *What are the odds?* I ask myself.

The anticipation of seeing him on Sunday lightens my mood. I don't get overly excited about dating, but this guy seems different, and I'm not sure why.

Sunday arrives, and my nerves have kicked into overtime; I am now dreading our first date. I do my best to shrug off the jitters, focusing instead on spending the afternoon with a guy I'm truly interested in. My closet floor is a mess, strewn with rejected outfits. I don't have anything suitable to wear. Everything's either too fancy or too casual. I can tell he's a jeans kind of guy, so I decide to play it safe.

I slide my legs into a pair of worn-out jeans, choose a fitted sweater, and finish with my favorite cowboy boots. There's no time to ponder any longer. The doorbell is ringing, leaving me only seconds to finalize hair, makeup, and outfit.

When I greet him at the door, I'm surprised to see that he has arrived in a Mercedes rather than his pickup truck. As we share a nervous first-date peck on the cheek as a greeting, he asks, "Would you mind if I checked on the water heater before we leave?"

"Please do!" I respond. The fact that he offers to check on his temporary repair is not lost on me. I've missed the comfort of a man around the house for some time.

Crossing over the Zakim Bridge, we soon enter Boston's notorious North End neighborhood, located at the edge of Boston Harbor. The Hanover Street sidewalks buzz with tourists and patrons despite the chilly end-of-winter temperature. The luscious smell of garlic permeates the air, a scent that instantly rejuvenates my memories of this Italian neighborhood and my younger, twenty-four-year-old self. It makes me feel slightly homesick for the chic city life I lived many years ago.

At twenty-four years of age, I had managed to switch from working long hours in a secretarial job to studying in the high-rise classrooms of Suffolk University, located in the prestigious Beacon Hill community and a stone's throw from the Boston Common. I gained as much knowledge living in this ethnic neighborhood as I did sitting in a college lecture hall. I loved how the two brought such diversity into my life. I was finally living my dream, even though I had arrived a bit late.

Throughout my early childhood, I'd identified naturally with the chain of command among my five siblings and was proud to be part of the lineup. But as I matured to twelve and thirteen years old, shortly after my grandmother's death, I found my relationship with my parents and siblings deteriorating, as I struggled to figure out who I was within the family. Meanwhile, my awkwardness intensified as I gained weight and lost confidence. I became sullen, wearing my hair long and letting the blonde strands hide my face, as I grew into my teen years. I missed the support of my recently deceased grandmother, who had made me feel so special in my house full of brothers and a baby sister.

I didn't get the sense that my presence contributed much of anything to the family mix. At an early age, I had sat quietly at family dinners while the chatter bypassed me. I never quite knew how to express myself or keep up with the banter.

Sensing my input wasn't missed, I began to retreat to my bedroom, finding comfort in my solitude. Slowly and without my intention, I fell into the background of this large, dynamic family. My status in the family did not change as we all grew up together. It seemed to me that I was branded early in life as the lost child, existing on the outer perimeter of the family circle.

My aimless wandering continued through high school, affecting my grades. At the same time, my friends put me on notice that I was not up to par to remain in their circle. There was no discussion. Their planned avoidance in the hallway was all they needed to do.

Over time, I withdrew from myself, becoming the master of disguise. I managed to hide myself for at least a few years before anyone noticed, but at that point I had become comfortable as an introvert.

I worked full-time after high school rather than attend college and regained my strength in my early twenties. At the age of twenty-four, I no longer wanted to be an observer, watching my siblings go off to private high schools and colleges while I stayed behind, working.

After months of deliberation, and having no idea how he would react, I mustered up the courage to ask my dad if I could follow my siblings' footsteps to college. I was living on my own and hadn't done much to instill his trust in me over the past few years, so I prepared for the worst and waited for the right time to approach him.

One evening, as he was eating dinner alone in the kitchen after a sixteen-hour workday, I started the conversation. "Hey Dad, "I've been thinking about going to college. I think it's time, and I really want to make a change."

At first, he responded with a blank stare, and then he did what he often did. He yelled for my mother. "Marni, could you please come down here?"

Oh, shit, I thought. *He's bringing in reinforcement. This isn't going to go well.*

"Stella thinks she might want to go to college," my dad said to my mother.

"What would you like to study?" my mother asked, one of her eyebrows rising a bit higher than the other.

"I don't know," I responded, my eyes looking downward. "I just know I don't want to live like this anymore."

So, my college trek began. I was a bit late in the game, but I still arrived in time to make it count. Within weeks of the conversation with my parents, I found myself moving into an adorable walk-up, one-bedroom apartment in the North End of Boston, a rental gift from my father, who, it turns out, was ecstatic that I was finally attending college. It was no surprise that I chose to live alone. I loved the apartment with its exposed-brick interior walls and a corner view of Boston Harbor. Located on the Freedom Trail, I would sit on my fire escape in the evenings, absorbing the energy of the city and smoking cigarettes while watching the tourists pass beneath me.

I entered college with exuberance. I was older and more mature than the other students, and I was so appreciative to be sitting in the classroom, ten floors up, looking out at the Boston skyline instead of punching a time card. I was engaged in classes that held my interest. I dove into my studies rather than just getting through them. For the first time in a long while, I felt accomplished, strong, and alive. I was finally an equal to my siblings, although my upgraded status was acknowledged with minimal fanfare.

Almost as if in unison, this was a turning point for my relationship with my mother. We began to rebuild together, putting the difficult teenage years behind us. Eventually, I stepped into her shoes as a mother myself, raising my own children alongside her. My mother, Marni, remains and will always be, my best friend and confidant.

My life had changed so quickly, and all it had taken was for me to initiate the change, to step out of my shadow and speak for myself. I never realized until the conversation with my parents that the power of change had been within my grasp all along. Unbeknownst to me, my parents had been waiting in the background for me to figure things out in my own time and on my own terms. I managed to do four years of college in three years' time, enjoying every moment of my classes and the city life I had grown to love.

It took two years of living in the North End before the shop owners began to call me by my name. The elderly butcher with the hearty laugh began saving me leftover portions of his homemade mozzarella, calling me Stella Sweetie as I passed by his shop in the mornings. The owner of a tiny corner restaurant often greeted me with takeout boxes of leftover specials from the evening's menu as I walked home from my summer night classes. I slowly began to take on the "edge" of the North End, adapting to its traditions and the cryptic Boston city accent as I transformed into a city girl.

Not much about the city intimidated me, except for the old-school pharmacist who owned one of the last existing mom-and-pop drugstores, located at the end of my street. He would scowl and convey to me, in Italian, his disapproval as he briskly slid my contraceptive prescription across the counter toward me. I dreaded those monthly trips.

Through the years, each time I returned to the North End, I was in awe that, no matter how much time had passed, the North End remained a timeless gem. The Boston skyline framed this ethnic Italian neighborhood with its spectacular cityscape, and the scent of garlic never grew old. Some of the restaurants that lined Hanover Street were so small that they held only four to five tables. A long line of hungry patrons waited outside for the next available seating, so they could indulge in the local culinary delights prepared with old-world recipes handed down from generation to generation.

Not knowing what restaurant Jake has chosen for our date, I am taken aback for a moment when he pulls up to valet parking at the Santo Osteria, my favorite restaurant in all of Boston. This man I barely know has my attention, as I keep in mind the subliminal messages sent to me the day he rang my doorbell.

Today the restaurant's large windows are cranked open just slightly, welcoming in the fresh, cool air along with the sound of street traffic. Young, homegrown Italian waiters recite menus with a perfect blend of Sicilian and Boston accents rolling off their tongues. The expressive hand gestures passed down from their elders are the final touch to a quintessential Italian presentation of their menu.

People tend to linger here, enjoying the whole experience that naturally fuses culture and cuisine into every bite. Those in the know skip the restaurant's desserts and instead take refuge in one of the famous local Italian bakeries along Hanover Street. Or they indulge in the local coffee houses that serve strong cappuccino, gelato, and fresh cannoli. I'm thrilled to once again be surrounded by old-world culture on this busy street I once called home.

Jake and I drink wine and talk for hours. Our conversation flows seamlessly and comfortably. Our bar stools move closer together as afternoon fades into evening with no sign of our first date slowing down. Jake tells me about his construction company and the immense success he is having with it. I notice he's a name-dropper, inserting high-profile executive clients' names, even though they don't add real value to the conversation. He does his best to make it clear that he is well connected.

I like the comfort of his arm draped around the back of my chair, along with the steady flow of appetizers. The caprese salad with homemade mozzarella and balsamic vinegar, fried calamari, and a seafood platter serve as our next course, along with more wine. Casually dining while getting to know each other, the two of us seem far more interested in our mutual attraction than in the delicious food being served.

Jake becomes somber as he speaks of his diagnosis of kidney cancer a few years prior. He fights back emotion as he describes being alone while dealing with his illness. He stares into my eyes as I talk about my kids and my family. For the two of us, no one else is in the room. We are fixated on each other and deep in conversation. The flow is natural, and the thrill is mutual. I don't want the date to end. I can tell he doesn't either.

Later in the evening, he drops me off, stopping his car in my driveway, leaning over to give me a lingering, soft, gentle kiss. I get out of the car and float up my front steps.

As I close the front door behind me, my cell phone buzzes with a text from Jake.

"When can I see you again?"

Chapter 3
Mid-March 2011

JAKE ARRIVES TWO HOURS earlier than his work crew on the day of the water heater installation. It is obvious to me why he has arrived so early—on a school day, with no children in the house—but I have no intention of sleeping with him, even though the house is empty, and we have time on our hands. I want to get to know him better. I need to know he's the real deal.

Chatting in my kitchen, we cover everything from life, to kids, to our history. I am more relaxed in his presence now, wearing a pair of old jeans and bare feet, sitting comfortably on a kitchen stool. Jake sits on the counter, dangling his legs so close that I can feel them brush gently against me. We are still strangers, getting to know each other, yet hoping to become lovers.

Just as I am contemplating whether to accept his advances, the doorbell rings and the arrival of his work crew conveniently saves me from deciding. For now, our rendezvous is a private affair. Both of us would like to keep it that way.

When the job is finished, he passes me in the hall, whispering into my ear an invitation to lunch. How can I refuse? Within fifteen minutes, the two of us are seated at the local hamburger hangout enjoying lunch, an afternoon cocktail, and each other's company.

Days later, with the momentum building swiftly, we head out to dinner again. This time it's to his past urban stomping ground. Boston's Back Bay neighborhood is geared toward the social and political elites, with its affluent brownstones that show off the multi-millionaire lifestyle. Ironically, it is also just a few blocks from the North End where I once lived. I find it romantically ironic that we lived in the same city simultaneously, less than a mile from each other.

Jake likes to take charge with our plans. His confidence is evident in his demeanor. We have a lot in common and the chemistry between us is off the charts, simmering each time we're together.

He's not the typical man of choice for me. A husky guy, he's tall, with strong arms that engulf me in heartfelt hugs. He's more rugged and less educated than the men I'm accustomed to, but his quick wit and humorous outlook on life have captured my attention. He works endlessly to promote himself and his accomplishments, showing me he is a proud man. I like a man of confidence.

Our Back Bay date is progressing just as the first outing did. Hand in hand, we stroll his old neighborhood before stopping for dinner at a small restaurant, Randall's Bar & Grill, with its old-world charm, influenced by the presence of the wealthy bow-tied regulars. Located below street level, it is an eatery that only the locals know about. We settle in at the dark oak bar that is smooth and shiny from years of applied lacquer. Both of us reaching out at the same time to hold the other's hand, casually chatting. Everything between us feels electric as we continue to explore our unchartered territory with ease.

Jake dives into his career history once more, framing it by explaining that he didn't go to college. Instead, he chose to work with his hands, a choice that appears to be serving him well. His popularity is obvious when former clients approach the bar to greet him. He takes time to speak to each of them, relishing his role as the local construction expert for socialites and big-business types. The bartender delivers another round of cocktails, and, as our evening continues, we have stars in our eyes.

What Jake lacks in vocabulary and education, he makes up for in charisma and financial success—which he boasts of perhaps a bit excessively. I'm not a big fan of digging into other people's finances, as I'd rather get to know people first. But he's eager to put it all on the table. I listen politely but offer no feedback. I'm more private, holding off and moving a bit slower into full financial disclosure.

Much to my surprise, that evening Jake sails into deeper waters, asking more personal questions: What kind of man do you like? Are you looking for a long-term relationship?

A bit thrown, I respond vaguely about my interests, not sure how to answer, because quite honestly, I am not looking for a certain type of guy at this point in my life. I recently ended a seven-year relationship, vowing to be happily single from that point forward. I find it somewhat alarming that I'm actually on a date so quickly, given my recent vow of abstinence, but here I am, surprising myself. It seemed to happen so naturally when Jake rang my doorbell for the first time.

Then the conversation turns to his own thoughts about what he's searching for in a relationship. "I want someone to worship me every night when I walk in the door."

His statement stops me in my tracks. But it doesn't stop me from an impulsive response: "Well, good luck with that."

I can feel his hand on my thigh tense as a shadow crosses his face. His disappointment in my response shows in his eyes ever so briefly, yet he recovers, and his sense of humor returns. Our meals arrive just in time for us to move on to a more enjoyable activity, dining and flirting with each other.

After my second martini, I excuse myself for a quick escape to the ladies' room to freshen up. Before entering, I turn around to find him behind me. We are alone for a moment, and he pulls me toward him for a kiss. I am flattered, but I quickly pull back, uncomfortable with public displays of affection. With a wink, he walks back to his seat, leaving us both smiling. After composing myself in the ladies' room, I cozy up to the bar, sitting a bit closer and becoming more captivated as the night wears on.

Just as on our first date, neither of us wants the evening to end. I know he is hoping for an invite when he drops me at home, but I withhold the invitation. I have two protective daughters inside. But more to the point, I still want to get to know him better, to be sure of who he is. I don't want to enter this relationship blindly. I am paying close attention to every detail, obeying the premonition sent to me on the day we met.

Not long after our first date, we begin to mingle with his friends. All of them appear to be professional and personable, but I sense a deeper insight from these friends I meet. I can't put my finger on it. They are well-educated, successful, corporate men and women who are filled with good-hearted questions aimed at me. They use humor to lighten the mood, but behind their jokes, I sense that they know another side of Jake. I'm uncertain how these friends blend with his style and interests.

It has been a whirlwind adventure since Jake first rang my doorbell, I now rush to be on time for our dinner dates and delay errands, which affects the household. Driving Zoey to her activities and keeping our schedules in order are taking their toll on me, leaving me to feel over-whelmed and pressed for time.

This particular evening, Jake is to pick me up at 6:30, but at 5:00, I'm still sitting in the driveway of Zoey's friend, waiting impatiently. Much to Zoey's surprise, I begin scolding her as she hops into the front seat. In the midst of exchanging words, I hear a loud *boom!* that rocks Zoey and me in our seats, instantly bringing us to a halt physically and verbally.

In my rearview mirror, I see the cause. In my haste, I have backed the car into a large tree. As if the car damage isn't bad enough, now both of us are frustrated with each other, and Zoey is embarrassed that it happened in her friend's driveway. The five-minute ride home isn't pleasant.

Finally, calm, we pull into our driveway to examine the damage. Out of the blue, as we're staring silently at the large dent and the broken bumper, Zoey starts smiling, which makes me grin at the absurdity of the last few minutes. "Geez, Mom! You almost took the tree down!"

"I know. What the hell!" I smile. "Who knew going five miles per hour could cause so much damage?"

Looking at the car hurts, but the humor helps to alleviate the pain, making me realize it isn't such a big deal after all. My beautiful Lexus, now tarnished with a smashed tailgate, needs extensive bodywork. This fender-bender has made me even more pressed for time, but I manage to get the girls fed and Zoey snuggled into my bed to watch TV and complete her homework, while I apply the finishing touches for date night with Jake.

The day after the accident, Jake calls midmorning, inviting himself over for a short visit. I scurry through the house, cleaning and tidying, just as he pulls into the front circular driveway. He enters the front door smiling and kisses my forehead.

We talk for a bit; I am trying to figure out the reason for his visit. He's got something on his mind, but I've not a clue what it might be. Mid-thought, he holds out the keys to his Mercedes, insisting that I accept his offer to drive his car until my car is fixed. Even better, he offers to take my Lexus to a body shop. My last long-term relationship was with a man who was stingy with his time and his support, making this gesture of Jake's something special. He's proving to be a kind man who likes to take care of things for a woman, something I had missed for a long time.

Riley defensively humps Jake's leg in retaliation when he steps toward me to place the keys into the palm of my hand. Then Jake lifts me into his arms and carries me into my bedroom. Riley follows us, nervous that someone is touching me, doing his best to protect me. But Jake has a different plan. He opens the front door to put Riley outside, leaving him to look back at me reluctantly, as if to say, "Are you okay with this, Mom?" Hanging his head in disappointment, Riley sits on the front stairs as if he's been put out to pasture.

Returning to my bed, Jake slowly undresses himself and then me. He's more interested in exploring than in the act itself. His hands are gentle, and his eyes are focused on mine. He whispers, "How does it feel to be with the last man you'll ever need?"

His question distracts me, creating an awkward moment of silence between us. I'm slightly uncomfortable with the insinuation that this is a lifelong encounter. This isn't the first time he's made comments to imply a sense of permanency between the two of us. I smile up at him, keeping my thoughts to myself as we intertwine in bed for the first time. This fabulous man I have become infatuated with is slowly working his way into my world.

We spend hours in bed, talking and curled up with each other. By two-thirty that afternoon, I realize I'm late to pick up Zoey at middle school.

When I get there, Zoey climbs into the Mercedes and looks at me. "Whose car is this, and what the hell happened to you? Your hair looks awful."

I just smile and laugh silently, thinking, *It was a marvelous day, the beginning of something special.*

Zoey quickly catches on that the car belongs to Jake. Changing her tone, she smiles. "Well, at least your boyfriend has good taste in cars."

Chapter 4
April 2011

THE REMAINING BROWN-TINTED snow clings defiantly to the earth, but the hiking paths show a glimmer of rejuvenation, peeking out from under a diminishing winter freeze. Riley and I set out to take our first celebratory hike of the season, breathing new life into our lungs as we rediscover the acres of conservation land and muddy trails that surround my backyard. Spring is proof that life goes on even after a harsh New England winter.

Each day, Riley waits patiently, looking for any sign from me that it is time for our walk. He's even more excited when Jake joins us, because he knows the hikes will be longer and deeper into the woods than I would venture alone. Riley loves these hikes so much that his entire face smiles. His eyes dance with anticipation at the mere jingle of his hiking collar.

His doggy bliss motivates me to hike with him every day, knowing that one missed day, while not a big deal to me, is an affliction to him. I am his world, and he is mine. I don't take my responsibility with him lightly. Jake is also falling in love with my silly dog; it pulls on my heartstrings as I watch them become better acquainted.

Spring also means that Jake's birthday is on the horizon, creating a conundrum for our newly established couple status. Something big for his birthday will appear to be exorbitant, while something obscure will look careless. After some thought, I arrive at the perfect solution. I'll share my favorite place with him, giving the gift of time spent together, as he has done for me. As his birthday approaches, I invite him to celebrate with Zoey and me in Naples, Florida. I'm usually much more guarded, rarely initiating such an invitation, but for some reason, it feels natural to ask.

For my family, all roads lead to Naples. We adapted to the Florida lifestyle twenty-five years ago when my parents purchased their first beach condominium overlooking the Gulf of Mexico. Since then, Naples has been my winter destination; I've vacationed there with my children year after year, and they've grown accustomed to our lavish oceanside vacations.

All these years later, Zoey, the baby of the family, still benefits from these vacations, while my two older kids, Harris and Julia, prefer to explore new destinations with their friends rather than tag along with their mom and baby sister.

"Ah, just a few perks of being the baby of the family," Zoey will often say with a smile.

Zoey and I arrive in Florida a few days early to allow for mother-daughter beach time, as I prepare for Jake's arrival. Zoey is settled in with her grandmother for the afternoon. I'm a bit nervous but excited about Jake's incoming flight.

There's something about meeting your new lover at the airport that sizzles with romance. He greets me at the baggage claim, lifting me off the ground and hugging me tightly.

Within forty-five minutes of leaving the airport, we check into his hotel and christen his room with the newness of us before making our first stop at my favorite beach bar. The Ritz-Carlton serves up the best cocktails and mango iced tea I've ever tasted. Let the birthday weekend begin!

With piña coladas in hand, we sit on the sand, me in my bikini top and him in his shorts, while the tropical breeze brushes our skin.

Lingering long after the beachgoers have gone, we lounge together, watching the sky take on a tropical orange hue. It is peace on earth in this part of the world at sunset.

Strolling the beach, we arrive at my family's condo. The elevator takes us to the twentieth floor, opening directly into the home, a space of upholstered walls and antique rugs. Jake is mesmerized by the ocean view that spans for miles before melting into the horizon. Sparkling diamonds glisten on the water as far as the eye can see.

My mom greets us warmly, wearing blue jeans and a warm smile. She is eager to meet this new man in my life. "Hi, my name is Marni, and I've heard so much about you," she says, greeting him like an old friend with a hug and air kisses.

It takes no time at all for him to turn on the charm, impressing her with his humor as they sit on the lanai. They admire the last remnants of the sunset that is slowly fading from orange to pink and then dusk before finally sinking silently into the ocean. Leaving the two of them to chat, I head to the shower, first checking in with Zoey, who is in her room.

Freshly showered, I choose a long, floral maxi skirt and black tank top, showing off my tanned shoulders. As I apply the finishing touches, Zoey bounces herself onto my bed to watch me get ready. Looking at her, I regret bringing Jake here for the weekend. She dislikes not having my undivided attention during our vacation time. I know she sees it as me choosing Jake over her, but that couldn't be further from the truth.

We fall into our regular chatter, talking about whatever silly things come to mind.

As I finish, she smiles and says sarcastically, "You look like crap, Mom."

"Thank you, Zoey. It's nice to know I can always count on you to boost my confidence."

She slaps me a high five, curling her fingers ever so briefly around mine, as she flashes me her beautiful smile.

"I love you, Zoey."

"Love you too, Mom."

Zoey and I are greeted by Jake's look of approval as I approach the lanai. He's relaxed, smiling, and pleased to be here. We share the remaining Merlot in his wineglass, as we take in the last of the ocean view. With final hugs from Zoey and my mom, Jake and I set out for the evening.

The maître d' seats us at an oceanfront table for two, perfect for continuing the flirtatious dance of getting to know each other on a more serious level. We dine on freshly caught seafood and French martinis. The ambiance of the open sky and Caribbean music make the entrées even more enticing.

The conversation turns once more to his successful contracting career and his plans for a more lucrative national approach to expanding his construction business, which is currently bursting at the seams. He speaks fondly of his daughter, a college student, and his son, whose passion lies in varsity lacrosse.

Early in the evening, I detect a sense of nervousness in Jake, and I'm not sure what all his boasting means.

"Next week, my boat will be in the water. It's a thirty-five footer, an expensive hobby but one I can't live without. I dock in the North End of Boston, so I have access to all the restaurants." He glides from one topic to the next. "I'm selling my ski house in New Hampshire. My kids and I outgrew it."

He works diligently throughout dinner to promote himself, fixated on talking about his wealth, homes, boats, career, and the new BMW he's ordering. I tend to be more of a listener than a talker, but, even so, just participating minimally in the conversation is somewhat difficult. In an effort to end the conversation, I let his comments slide without offering any follow-up questions, filing away the comments in my mind.

By the time the waiter delivers the bananas flambé, the conversation has shifted back to a more casual tone, which suits me just fine.

CHAPTER 4

Our three sun-filled days together are nothing less than spectacular. Jake and I stroll the beach each morning, walking for miles, searching for seashells and wading in and out of the salty water. I wrap my arms around his shoulders as I float on his back, breathing in the scent of his sweat mixed with sunscreen and tasting the saltwater on his lips. Our bodies tan darker by the hour as we linger at the shore under a beach umbrella until it is near dinnertime.

In the evening we watch the sun set, posting nauseating "I'm in love" photos on social media. Every moment together, we make sure we are within touching distance, walking hand in hand.

As night washes over us, we make love on the beach, lying together on the sand with arms and legs entangled. We listen to the waves caress the shore and talk about anything that comes to mind. Everything between us flows smoothly and effortlessly. It just fits perfectly.

On our last day together in paradise, Zoey and I come out to our beach spot to find a large heart drawn in the sand around our chairs, framed with beautiful shells. And my handsome boyfriend is waiting for me, holding my favorite iced tea and Zoey's strawberry smoothie.

In contrast, these three days can't pass quickly enough for Zoey. She has become increasingly agitated; there is no way of pleasing her. Instead, she spends most of her time with my mom, shopping and ignoring me.

At this point, I am between a rock and a hard place, trying to make everyone happy. Zoey's teenage hair flip and eye-rolling leave me torn inside, feeling selfish that I initially thought this was a good idea. I want to spend time with both of them, but I am the only person with that agenda in mind. Each of them wants all of me.

After we drop off Jake at the airport, Zoey's irritation subsides, and we sail back into calmer moments for the remainder of our vacation. Yet I am conflicted after this Naples trip.

The plane ride home with Zoey is quiet. In retrospect, I can see she was aware this man was special to me, a fact that might have intimidated her from the start. She and Julia had been uncomfortable with my post-divorce relationships in the past, despite the fact that their dad and I had been divorced for twelve years. In full disclosure, I have had my share of relationship blunders since then, so the fact my daughters are wary is understandable.

How can I blame them for their anger toward me? I have never been a child of divorce, as they have. Who am I to say that my daughters are wrong for the way they feel? This situation frustrates me, yet I feel tremendous guilt at the same time, leaving no room for resolution within myself. I am attempting to move on with my adult life, while taking care of my family at the same time, hoping the two can balance without being problematic. Single parenting brings on a whole new dimension of mistakes and challenges, including post-divorce dating.

After giving it much thought, I wish I hadn't been upset with Zoey and had been more insightful on her behalf. Bringing Jake to Naples was a selfish idea for me and one I regret, because my daughter was trying to tell me she wasn't ready. Zoey was protecting herself and me in her own way, and I responded by being annoyed with her. I ignored her efforts, when she deserved better from me.

I recall one of my favorite quotes, which I apply to these types of situations with my children: "A mother is only as happy as her saddest child."

Less than one week after returning from Naples, I have one of those days when chaos reigns. *Fire in the hole!* I think to myself.

Zoey and Julia have formed an alliance, being angry about Jake's presence and leaving me outnumbered. As usual, the girls feed off each other, as things escalate into a tirade. It's two daughters against one parent, the kiss of death for peace in our house.

Not a day goes by that I do not realize my immense love for my kids. However, every now and then, they push me too far, forcing me to crack under pressure. It is times like these when I use my wild card, a rescue phone call to their father, my ex-husband, Corey. I can always count on him to pick up the kids, allowing me a much-needed break from their shenanigans.

Corey walks through the front door to find the situation has escalated. In the foyer, Zoey has defiantly poured her petite body into the laundry basket along with the dirty clothes, yelling and announcing to the world that she will not be leaving the house with her father under any circumstances.

Zoey's tantrum takes center stage, while Julia points defiantly to me and says to her dad, "See what Mom's done? She's got Zoey all upset again!"

Finding no logic to anything he's seeing, Corey quietly picks up Zoey, still sitting in the laundry basket, and carries her out of the house with her arms flailing. Julia follows, making certain to exit with her signature door slam that rattles me far more than it rattles the house. It's times like this when I truly appreciate the fact that Corey is still in my corner during the rough-and-tumble periods. Regardless of our divorce, which has wavered between good and not so good over the years, we are still a family. He will always hold a place in my heart as my first love and the father of my children.

After the infamous door slam, once he senses the coast is clear, Riley comes out of hiding to sit next to me. His look of confusion says it all: *What the heck just happened here?*

We sit together on the steps that curve softly up to the second floor, where my kids have slept since they were small children. I think defensively, *How many times have I climbed these stairs to say good night to my babies? How many times have I watched them come down these same stairs for breakfast, proms, and Christmas mornings? These kids are my life.*

I pet Riley's head, watching him tilt it from side to side, as he looks at me with his sturdy gaze and big brown eyes, pretending to understand the words I'm mumbling to him. Riley and I have our own language, so I answer for him in his own silly tone. The dialog between us goes on until he tires of me and scratches at the front door to be let outside.

My heart is weary as silence falls on the house. I can't help but be shaken when there's discord in my home. It's rare to have the house to myself for any extended period of time. Instead of sitting, I vacuum the entire house to burn off some of the negative energy. I shower early, put on my PJs, and make popcorn for dinner.

By eight o'clock I am snuggled in bed, with Riley resting on the pillow next to me. It's just the two of us watching TV and dozing off and on. I watch out of the corner of my eye as Riley inches closer and closer to the bowl of popcorn, waiting for me to snooze once more so he can lick the butter from the bottom of the bowl.

At nine-thirty my phone rings. I assume it's one of the girls calling to apologize, but instead it's Jake's voice I hear. He's eager to offer me an open invitation to stay with him for a few days while I'm temporarily childless. It is a nice gesture on his part, but there's no chance I'll be leaving my spot in bed with Riley and even less of a chance that I'll be inviting him over. I am exactly where I want to be, and I am not interested in company.

I wake the next morning to the sun rising through the windows with renewed energy, a quiet house, and a clean kitchen. As wonderful as the peace and quiet might sound, I prefer the pitter-patter of teen-age feet and their untidy presence, including the dirty dishes in the sink—even though I scold them constantly for the messes they make.

The silence brings me to a new perspective. Today is a new day. The kids are safe with their dad. What am I going to do? Sit at home in an empty house and feel terrible? This is a rare opportunity for me to take some time to do as I please.

After two more text invitations from Jake, he succeeds in persuading me to pack up my client files, laptop, and Riley and head over to his house for a few days.

Just south of the New Hampshire border, his home is a man's abode that he built himself. By day I work from my laptop, as I lounge by his backyard pool in the spring sunshine. In the evening, Jake serves candlelit dinners on his porch. Simple salads, fresh tuna, and wine are plenty to keep our stomachs full and our minds engaged in conversation. Being away from home is a nice diversion from the argument with my girls, but my kids never leave my mind. I miss them. The discord between us interferes with every thought I have.

This visit to Jake's home unexpectedly opens my world to many activities I know little of but am eager to learn about. His custom Harley-Davidson motorcycle is his favorite, and it soon becomes mine also. I quickly find I adore riding on the back of the bike, holding on tightly to his waist, enjoying the view, and feeling the breeze in my face as my head clears.

My camera dangles from my neck. I take photographs and capture the open-air countryside. I can't get enough of the farmhouses and the landscape, with row upon row of early crops peeking up from the earth. For the first time since the argument with my girls, I begin to unwind.

Riding deeper through the winding country roads into New Hampshire, we stop at roadside breakfast joints that serve up huge pancakes with homemade maple syrup. We prefer old-fashioned country diners, where the specialty is deep-fried pickles and ice cream frappés. Evening rides on the Harley take us to wine bars, where we snack on appetizers and share glasses of Merlot. The two of us are happily eating our way through the countryside. His bike brings me a serenity I have never experienced before. My admiration grows deeper for him and his bike.

He keeps his four-wheel quads parked in his backyard, ready to ride off into the woods at a moment's notice. I want to ride them as soon as I see his neighbors have quads too. They speed out from the woods, using Jake's backyard as a shortcut, and wave to us on the porch as they zoom past.

The next day, I take my first ride on a quad, driving much too carefully through the woods. Jake shows me how to ride up steep hills, through streams, and over railroad tracks and bridges. It doesn't take long for me to learn how to speed around corners, riding the bumps standing rather than seated. I am covered in dirt and squealing with laughter.

We stay out for the entire day, riding the wooded trails and discovering hidden paths and back roads. He is a patient teacher, who knows how to turn a day in nature into a whimsical, romantic memory. He packs picnic lunches that we eat under a large oak tree, taking in country views of the river.

We stop in the middle of the woods, where the sun is shining through the tallest of trees. He shuts off his quad and climbs onto the back of mine. The warmth of his body keeps the chill away, as I lean back comfortably against his chest. We talk, laugh, and eat granola bars, breathing in the fresh air. Both of us are content in this simple moment.

Dusk has fallen by the time we get back to his house. We devour all the leftovers in his fridge, ending the day with a shared glass of wine and a grilled cheese sandwich on his candlelit porch. A shared hot shower washes off the grime and then it's early to bed, where we make love and then hold hands through the night as we sleep.

I am learning that every day with Jake is an adventure. When we awake early the next morning, both of us sore and tired from riding the quads the day before, he nudges me to rise for an early morning paddle on the river. Toweling my wet hair after my shower, I peek out the front window to see him securing two kayaks in the back of his pickup truck. Feeling rushed, I pull my hair into a ponytail, and we are off for another day of fun!

Not sure where we are heading, yet trusting that he will take care of everything, I roll down the truck window to enjoy the morning breeze. I have never kayaked before and am a bit unsure whether I can pull it off without embarrassing myself. But after some quick instructions on land, he loads me into the kayak and pushes me off into the river, leaving me no choice but to paddle.

The river is miles long, complete with old ivy-covered bridges, with water so crystal clear that I can see the plant life and turtles beneath me as I paddle. Jake is strong, making it a challenge for me to keep up with him, but he always circles back, leaning into my kayak for a kiss and to recite random historical facts about the river.

Paddling along with the sun tanning us both, we come up on an old stone bridge covered in moss. Our kayaks hooked together with his foot, we make loud sounds that echo under the bridge, laughing to hear the sounds come back. In unison, we look up to see a plane circling overhead and wonder why it is flying so low—then we see colorful parachutists jumping from the plane. Their laughter fills the air as they swirl overhead and disappear, landing beyond the trees near a small airport. We watch in awe of it all as we hold hands, letting the water current carry us.

I hadn't had such active dates before I met Jake. He knew a little bit about everything, and he was a patient teacher, who offered me his full attention every day. Everything he did was to engage me and to teach me new things, showing me his world. I liked what I saw. Slowly, I began to fall more deeply in love with the outdoors, while falling in love with him at the same time.

I had grown tired of the wine-and-dine dates that were so popular in the post-divorce dating scene. Jake was a different type of guy, showing me a far different kind of romance than I was accustomed to. Instead of presents, he gave me the gifts of time and nature. Whatever I asked for, he delivered. Whatever I spoke of, he agreed. Whatever activity I wanted to learn about, he taught me. We existed as one, always in close proximity to each other. We slept with our bodies glued together, in tune physically and emotionally.

It was easy for people to see from afar—from any distance—that we were lovers. This relationship was blossoming into something much more than I had imagined.

A doting father, Jake has sole custody of his two children. His fifteen-year-old son, Dylan, and his eighteen-year-old daughter, Natalie, breeze in and out of the house, happy in their lives and bubbly with their discussions. I like them. They are different from my kids, as they have been raised by a single dad in a tight-knit, blue-collar community.

His talkative kids are kindhearted, inquisitive, and accepting of my presence with their dad.

As the week progresses, my perception of Jake and his children begins to shift. They are a happy family of three, but I am surprised to hear vulgarity in their conversations and direct insults aimed at Dylan. Jake and Natalie find humor in calling Dylan names when he hesitates to participate in the conversation. They laugh and call him "retard" and "Einstein," dramatically collapsing in laughter at the slightest misstep on Dylan's part. His humiliation is evident. Oftentimes he seems okay with the negative attention. Most of the time he does his best to smile through it. Honestly, it isn't the kids I am judging. I place the judgment on their father, who allows—and even encourages—the teasing.

These unusual conversations flow freely at home, in restaurants, and in stores. Even when they play badminton in the backyard, they shout for all the neighbors to hear, "Fuck you, fucking retard!" It is endless. The terms *douche*, *stupid*, and *shitfuck* are recited as common dialog. They like to refer to objects as whores.

"Hey, open up that whore and get the milk out."

I have never heard anyone call a refrigerator a whore. It is a hard thing to watch unfold. Being a part of this makes me homesick for my kids, where there is more of a respectful separation between parent and children.

I'm not saying that I don't swear. I do, but this is far more extreme. I don't like it at all. I try to focus on all the positive aspects of this loving family, but the extent of the vulgarity is a hard thing for me to ignore.

I wrestle with the discovery that Jake and I have different parenting models. Finally, I muster up the courage to speak to him about the language, but I am met with nothing more than a grin, because Jake doesn't see anything wrong with the language. Given the beginning stage of our relationship, I hold out hope. *After all, we are only dating,* I remind myself. *It's not my business. It's possibly an overreaction on my part.* Nevertheless, I stow it away in my memory for future reference.

Natalie and Dylan's mom is a welcome presence in their lives and in Jake's home. I met her one evening when she visited her kids and thought she was lovely and soft-spoken. We chatted with ease, as she quickly fell in love with Riley.

I like his kids. They love each other very much. They are a team. They are blue-collar tough like their dad. Natalie controls the dynamics of their family triangle and has clearly played that role for many years. She possesses a humorous personality and has true love in her heart for her family.

I bond quickly with Dylan, a quiet, tall boy. I can tell he has a lot to say, but a finite window of time in which to state it before he is cut off. It appears he has been raised in a difficult situation, being laughed at but loved deeply.

My hope is that someday Dylan realizes he is the true leader of that small family. He is genuinely kind and smarter than they recognize. He has a silent determination and humbly beholds an immense sense of personal pride.

Growing weary of being away too long, I am ready to get home to my own family and leave Jake with his. As frustrated as I have been with my daughters' behavior, I miss my kids terribly. I have my own daily challenges to deal with at home.

On the last morning of my visit, I wake up in Jake's bed, my mind filled with a to-do list after my week away. Turning to stretch, I look over to see him standing in his closet in his underwear, grinning from ear to ear.

As I shake the sleep out of my head, he asks, "How about you and your kids move in here with us? There are plenty of bedrooms. The house is big enough. You and the kids would love it here." He looks silly and in love as he rushes over to the bed and scoops me into his arms.

As preposterous and charming as the proposition is, I decline to answer, knowing that the answer will be a solid no. I hug him back and nuzzle his neck for one last caress before packing my overnight bag and heading home with Riley. My daughters are due home by ten o'clock this morning, and I want to be there to greet them.

As Riley and I drive off, Jake stands on his front steps, waving good-bye. Within seconds, I receive a text, Jake's first "I love you." I don't respond, savoring the moment cautiously. My smile is bright the entire way home; I'm happy to have had a few days away with my lover in his space. I am delighted at the prospect of seeing my kids and thrilled to see Riley enjoying his ride, as he hangs his head out the window. Life is good.

Chapter 5
May 2011

THE RESTAURANTS AND SHOPKEEPERS along Newbury Street have replenished their outdoor gardens with my favorite blue and white hydrangeas, bringing the city sidewalks to life. Despite my blessed suburban existence, I still love spending time in this beautiful city of mine.

Jake likes to frequent small boutique hotels in Boston, and tonight is no different. The evening begins with an afternoon text from him. "Meet me in room 605 at the Boston Copley Hotel today at 4:00 p.m. Pack a bag and stay the night with me."

I prepare the house for Julia and Zoey, feed Riley, and make my way into the city.

The historically charming and well-preserved Boston Copley Hotel has been frequented by presidents and wealthy aristocrats dating back to 1891. The thumbprint of the architecture takes me back through time, as the small antique elevator makes its way to our sixth-floor room. Jake greets me at the door with a kiss, a glass of Merlot, and a bright, happy smile.

The room is small yet refined in detail. The tall windows reaching to the ceiling are framed by creamy white, wispy drapes just waiting for the opportunity to catch a breeze. An upholstered window seat invites guests to enjoy the city view. The glossy hardwood floors are stained a dark brown and a large crystal chandelier hangs directly over the bed, centering the room like a jeweled crown. Lit candles and poured wine bode well as the introduction to our night of romance.

Wasting no time, we fall into bed together, now comfortable and familiar with each other, yet still discovering. Lying in each other's arms, we drink wine, always sharing the same glass. We talk of our hopes and dreams, still high on our new love affair and mutually aware that we are falling in love.

The room is too special to leave unattended, and so is the freshness of our relationship. We relish the time as if we haven't seen each other in ages. We order room service, dining leisurely in bed on fruit-and-cheese platters, hamburger sliders, truffle fries, and strawberry parfait.

For such a romantic evening, I am surprised when he mentions his finances again. *Now?* is all I can think of at that moment.

He turns onto his side, looking into my eyes as he speaks, "I can take good care of you. Provide a really nice life for you . . . for us."

Despite my silence, he continues. I smile warmly, nodding politely. I want to show him I am impressed, while at the same I reach for the phone to call room service for another bottle of wine. It's my attempt at leaving the conversation behind us.

One thing is certain: the man is direct, and he knows what he wants. I'm flattered that he is falling in love with me, and I am ecstatic to be falling in love with him too. I can't remember the last time I felt so comfortable with a man or when a man has been so kind and generous. It's not only with city rendezvous and country afternoons but with his time spent teaching me new things and his eagerness to help me with any request I make. I am fortunate to be with such a successful, loving man who is eager to be a partner. I hear his message loud and clear.

We make our way out of bed, moving over to the window seat as the evening sets in. As I lounge back, my upper body fits perfectly against his chest. His thighs wrap comfortably around my hips. His shins and bare feet are tangled up with mine. We sit silently for a while, just resting together and watching the city life pass by.

On the sidewalks below, people move at their own pace in different directions. The cars surge past, honking, in a hurry to get somewhere. But not us. I, in my baby-blue lace bra and white silk pajama bottoms, and he, in a hotel bathrobe, are content right here, watching the activity of the city unfold from six floors up. It is a lovely evening, like every other time we've been together. We laugh for hours, make love once more, and finally fall asleep holding hands.

Morning arrives much too quickly. We wake to sunlight streaming through the window and the morning city sounds creeping up from the sidewalks below. Before I'm fully awake, room service is knocking on our door with an enormous breakfast of eggs, toast, fruit, pastry, coffee, and tea. Even with all the food we consumed the night before, I am famished, ready for breakfast in bed.

I don't want this exquisite romantic night with my lover to end. I want to stay in this room, basking in the bay window for another day with him, but I have too many things to do today. Unfortunately, I have to leave this dreamy state of mind and our lovers' bed.

I quickly shower, flip my wet hair into a sloppy bun, give him a long kiss goodbye, and fight him off as he tries to pull me back to bed. I grab my overnight bag and leave the hotel, feeling loved.

A sunny spring morning greets me as I step outside to find the valet waiting for me at the curb, with a smile and a cheery, "Good morning, Mrs. Jacobs." He holds open my car door. As I pull away, my phone buzzes with a message from Jake. "I love you. Can't wait to see you tonight."

I thread the Mercedes into the morning city traffic, taking back roads and alleyways to Storrow Drive, expertly maneuvering the roads to stay ahead of the daily commuters. With the music playing and a clean morning breeze flowing through the open sunroof, I buzz past the cherry trees along the Charles River at a brisk speed, heading for home.

Chapter 6
Summer 2011

CELEBRATING THE SUMMER MONTHS together, Jake and I split our time between his house and mine. Being with him takes stamina. He's generally active and always looking for things to do. The fire pit roars in the evenings. A wonderful cook, he is eager to show off his grilling skills to my girls. Riley stands at attention, waiting patiently for Jake to throw him juicy pieces of steak from the grill, which he catches in his mouth. Oftentimes a quick ride on the Harley through town on a warm summer night is in order; we explore the backroads wherever we go. With the exception of my girls' continuing animosity about my relationship with Jake, I am otherwise happy to have met this man.

The mere mention of an item on my bucket list thrusts him into action. Kayaking down the Saco River in the White Mountains of New Hampshire has been my wish. The next Saturday we are on the road at sunrise for the two-hour drive. Seated comfortably next to him in the passenger seat, in my oldest, comfiest sweatshirt, I am ready for the scenic country drive to North Conway, New Hampshire, and another engaging adventure.

Within two hours, we are dropping our kayaks into the sparkling cold water of the Saco River and heading downstream for the 7-mile trip. I am giddy with excitement. It doesn't take long to join the momentum of hundreds of other kayakers and tubers who consider this day trip to be a holiday of sorts, a floating party on the river. Everyone is in a celebratory mood. Couples, groups of friends, and entire families of tubers pass us. They've tied their tubes together, so their group doesn't get separated, dragging their six-packs of beer behind them in the icy river.

Animal lovers bring their dogs, putting them in the back seats of their kayaks, to partake in the downstream ride with their humans. The dogs periodically jump into the water to stay cool, dog-paddling in pace with their kayaks until their owners pull them back in. Teenagers camping at RV parks along the river stand knee-deep, fishing, waving, and shouting to the folks in tubes floating by to throw them cans of beer. Camaraderie on the river is evident as we continue downstream, all of us forming a bond for the day.

Jake paddles beside me, guiding my kayak, chatting, and calling out greetings to others as they pass us. We let the current gently guide us downstream, at times with no effort at all, allowing us the luxury of dangling our fingers in the water while drifting slowly downstream without a care in the world. It takes over four hours to complete the trip, but it ends much too soon, even though we are both sunburned and tired.

As we pull the kayaks out of the water, I throw my arms around him. "That was so much fun! I love you."

Jake stops in his tracks when he hears the words from me for the first time. "I love you too," he says, beaming.

We smile for days after that kayaking trip. I loved every minute of it, and I love him.

The summer just wouldn't be complete without the days spent on his boat, another new activity he brought into my world. Every time we find an opportunity to sneak away, we can be found floating on Boston Harbor. I have no complaints about being in the designated spot next to him, with his arm draped casually on my shoulder as he navigates. We clearly both feel as though we have no beginning and no end to the other.

If time allows, with our parenting schedules, we venture out of the harbor to follow the coastline. Headed north toward the town of Marblehead, we love to gaze at the oceanfront homes, picking out our favorite mansions.

The open water is where we enjoy complete privacy, dropping anchor in our secluded part of the ocean, sunbathing nude, and dining on fruit salad and homemade sandwiches, while the gentle sway of the boat lulls us into short naps together under the afternoon sun.

Fresh lobsters are pulled from the traps. We grill them on the back of the boat for our sunset dinner. Docking at Deer Island, one of my favorite stops, we search for sea glass and shells along the shore, returning to the marina in time to admire the Boston skyline light up into the night.

Our existence is far simpler and more natural than past relationships I have been in. There's no drama and no chaos. There is no loss for words nor any awkward silences between us.

Our hikes through country trails on cooler weekends are always on the agenda—me with my camera in hand to capture the landscape, he with his humor to keep us laughing, and Riley following along with us, as usual. We picnic on the tailgate of his truck by the river bend to watch the turtles sun themselves on the warm rocks. I have become enamored with the outdoors. He makes me feel safe. I want to do more with him by my side.

Both of us have been full-time single parents for many years. My children are busy and happy. Our daily lives are caught up in the routine of early morning commutes to three different private schools, sports, homework, and family dinners. Our hectic schedules make these relaxing moments with Jake even more special.

It's nice to set aside small pockets of private time for Jake and me, but at the end of each day, whether it be at my house or his, we both favor having our kids around us, one way or another. We understand it's a delicate situation for all. My preference is to not force a union between the five kids, nor do I feel we should compel them to accept us as a couple. These things take time, and their acceptance should be earned, not demanded.

"Leave it be," I say.

It's not the worst thing in the world to have separate pockets of our lives. He has his family and I have mine. I'm okay with that. I'm not a big believer in the concept of blending families. Past attempts to blend my kids into a current relationship have proven to be an epic failure. I like knowing that parts of my life are separate from his. I believe it to be a healthy way to live post-divorce.

As the summer passes, Jake persists in bringing up the subject of moving in together. Sitting on the bow of the boat one evening, the gentle rocking lulling us into serenity, he begins again. "Move in with me. You can do whatever you want with the house. Open checkbook. It's yours to do with what you wish."

I have become accustomed to avoiding these comments, and I do my best to dodge it again today. "My kids are happy where they are. I'm not moving my kids out of their house," I say with a twinge of irritation in my voice. "Please, Jake. We've only known each other a few months. Can we stop having this conversation?" This topic is draining me. The silence lingers a bit longer than is normal for these conversations.

Relationships often elude me, or perhaps I've made choices in the past that didn't serve me well. I want to get it right from this point forward; that is, on my own terms and with a timeline I am comfortable with. So, whenever possible, I steer away from talking about our future together. Living for the moment suits me just fine. I love where we are now—spending a romantic summer together and learning more about each other on a deeper level, instead of deciding whose house to live in, which couch to keep, and whose parental rules to follow.

Weeks pass, and summer draws to a close. The warm breeze changes ever so slightly, giving notice that shorter days and cooler temperatures are imminent. My thoughts turn to nesting and settling in for the winter. His talk of moving in together continues, and I'm still using my status quo defense. "We're together all the time anyway, so why change it now?"

But my plea for immunity is losing strength. We have grown close over the summer, and I know deep down that this relationship is unlike any other I've ever had. He has put me on a pedestal, and he goes out of his way to show me that he's a man I can trust.

After Natalie moves out of state, Jake changes direction by suggesting that he and his son move into my house, so I don't have to relocate my children. He gets excited about renovating things in my home, planning for a new kitchen, and evaluating each room for things that need repair. He has already fixed so many things in the house without asking—a thrill for a single woman with a large house to maintain. The landscaping has never looked better. The Mercedes, now mine, is maintained, washed, and filled with gas each week. We are together more than we are apart, and my daughters are slowly warming to his presence.

He has torn down unwanted walls in the house, and, in the process, he has begun to dismantle the emotional wall I have built over the years. He is opening my mind to the belief that love is a good thing. It's nice having a man around the house, and I am becoming accustomed to being a couple, something I didn't fully experience in my last long-term relationship.

Yet I continue to raise all the reasons why we shouldn't live together. How will our kids react? We are so happy just as we are! There's no doubt I am in love with this man, but I'm also feeling a bit confused and despondent at the same time, given this relentless pressure to move in.

Despite my apprehension, by the end of the summer we agree to a trial run, with the promise that marriage isn't an option and he will move back to his house if things don't work out. It is a compromise I feel comfortable with. And so, we agree to share the same front door.

Chapter 7
Labor Day 2011

ONE FINAL COOKOUT IS in order for Jake and Dylan's last night at their home. It's a celebration of sorts to mark our transition to roommates. We wake up together the next morning to the inevitable moving day.

Leading up to that day, I have broached the subject about organizing the move. With a wave of his hand, he has cut me off, telling me not to worry. But today, as I'm facing this in real time, I'm apprehensive all over again. The move seems so haphazard. It's not my style. I'm a planner, an organizer, a wrapper, and a packer.

As I look around his house on this morning, all I can see is a mess. I'm clueless as to how he's going to accomplish a move of this magnitude today. Nothing is packed or organized. He hasn't hired a truck or a mover to help him. Instead, he's randomly throwing things into the back of his truck. The closets are filled to the brim. There are no packing boxes to be found. He's casually leaving so much behind.

Feeling myself going into panic mode, I decide to head home and prepare for their arrival. I need to distance myself from this end of the move. I need space to think before he and Dylan arrive with their life packed into the back of his pickup truck. Feeling distressed, I pull out of his driveway, heading for home, thankful for the peaceful ride with Riley.

I drive along, talking things through with Riley as he rests his head on my shoulder, listening to every word. Everything is okay so long as Riley is close to me. But today he senses something. He leans in closer to me, sniffing my hair, watching my every move for a signal, and breathing down my neck as I drive.

Halfway home, I receive a random text from Jake. He's upset that Zoey left dishes in his kitchen sink last night after the cookout. "WTF with Zoey's dishes in the sink. Really?"

I ignore the text and keep driving. A few minutes later, another text comes through and then another, with each text becoming increasingly graphic. I'm baffled that he's so angry. *He's been living in a cluttered mess for years, so what's the big deal about a few dishes in the sink on moving day?* I shake my head, irritated and convinced it must be his anxiety about moving day—we're both on edge. And so, it begins.

Once home, I take a breath, trying to process his text messages while drinking my iced tea. The flavor of the tea and the chill of the ice cubes comfort me as they do every morning. *Where did his anger come from? Why the trivial conversation about two dishes in the sink? Why the focus on Zoey? She's my daughter, and she's off-limits to him. What in the world would bring on this tirade?*

I'm relieved to have the house to myself but overcome with my own anxiety about the texting and the prospect of moving day. I wander around the house, preparing for their arrival, but something in me isn't feeling right, and it grows in my gut. I retreat to my sanctuary, my master bathroom, where I sit on the side of the tub to contemplate my uneasiness. I feel queasy as I glance out my picture window to see his enormous, old Jacuzzi tub he had delivered yesterday. It takes over the entire bluestone patio. I hate it. *Damn it! Why did I agree to put the Jacuzzi on the patio? I don't even like Jacuzzis.*

I try to see beyond my frustration about the Jacuzzi and focus on the serenity of my beautiful backyard, but I still can't shake the tension.

CHAPTER 7

The green lawn spills into acre upon acre of wooded conservation land, filled with late-summer blooms of purple heather. If you're lucky, you can catch a glimpse of an occasional grazing deer.

What am I feeling? Fear of commitment? Anxiety? It's fear of something—that's for sure! Never have I felt so many negative emotions all at the same time. I wonder about the meaning of the message I am receiving at this moment. I wish these messages would be more descriptive. My thoughts bring me to my knees in front of the toilet, gasping for breath and holding back.

My conscience is churning inside me. So much is happening at once that I can't think straight. *Is this a panic attack?* I've never had one before. It sure feels like one. Moving day jitters, angry texts over dishes, disorganization, and second thoughts accumulate to a complete loss of my senses. I hate this feeling, and I never want to feel it again.

Damn! There's no more time to think. I hear his pickup truck pull in. I'm not sure why, but I tiptoe to the window and peek out cautiously. I see his truck filled to the brim with his belongings, piled on top of one another and tied down with rope.

Instead of pulling into the driveway, he drives over the grass and into the backyard. It's the first time anyone has ever done that, but I realize at this moment that there are going to be a lot of firsts with this new living arrangement.

My stomach is doing flips. Instead of greeting him, I close my bathroom door and sit on the cool tile floor with my back against the door, trusting he will know enough to allow me a bit of private space. I've lived in this house for fifteen years, and, for the first time, I wish the door to the master bath had a lock. I've never felt I needed one until now.

Moments later I hear a knock on the bathroom door.

"Are you okay?" he asks through the door.

"Yeah, I'm fine. I just need a minute. I'll be out in a bit."

Instead of waiting, Jake gently pushes open the door. My bottom slides across the tile as he steps in.

Chuckling, he asks, "What are you doing?" Sitting down next to me, he can see the tension I'm feeling. Reaching for my hand, he says, "Everything's going to be okay," making no mention of the angry texts he sent earlier and offering no apology for attacking my daughter with insults.

"I'm not so sure," I say. "You spouted off about Zoey today for no reason. Your house is a mess, and you insult my daughter for leaving dishes in the sink. Is this how things are going to be? Keep your comments away from my daughter. She's off-limits to you."

He smiles as he puts his arm around me, speaking softly. "I'm sorry, Stella. It's an important day, and I'm stressed out. You know how much I like Zoey. She's a cool kid. It won't happen again."

The silence in the room can be cut with a knife. I choose my next words carefully. "Jake, your house is a mess. I didn't know the extent of it until I woke up there today and saw the chaos of the move. Your basement is so disheveled that you can't even walk through it—there are nails and screws all over the floor. Your closets are so full that you can barely shut the doors. It's too much for me—you can't bring that mess here."

He appears insulted but brushes away my words with a wave of his hand, keeping his composure and trying to console me, as if I need to have the situation clarified.

"It's okay for couples to disagree. I have no intention of bringing a mess to this house. I've hired a crew to clean out the things I've left behind. I've already got my house rented to a friend who is getting a divorce. A few thousand dollars of rent money every month for you to use any way you want. It's going to be okay, Stella. No worries." Another silence ensues before he asks, "Stella, do you want me here?"

I reply softly, "I'm not sure. I think it's too soon."

He waits for a different answer from me, which doesn't come. He points to the backyard, where Dylan is unpacking the pickup truck. Watching Dylan fills me with guilt about my indecision. I remember the basement Jake has rebuilt for Dylan to live in at my house. He has his own private suite with a bedroom, TV room, full bath, and a private entrance. It's perfect for Dylan, who will face a new school, home, and family. There are lots of changes today, bringing on an equal amount of stress for all of us. My mind is swirling with angst about so many things; I can't coherently piece together a response.

Jake kisses my forehead, reassuring me that things will be drama free. "Just like we talked about, hon. A trial period and then we can decide where to go from there. I'll do whatever makes you comfortable." He strokes my hair and holds my hand. His words calm me as I begin to breathe once more.

My mood lightens as move-in day continues through the afternoon. Jake works around the house, repairing small things that need fixing. My cabinet doors no longer squeak, and the door screens slide open effortlessly. My front steps are no longer loose, and the plumber is called to inspect the basement pipes. His efforts calm my nerves to a small degree, as I make attempts to manage where their belongings will go. I soon realize they're putting their furniture where they see fit, so I stay out of the way, trying not to appear too territorial.

My beloved leather couch is moved and replaced with his beige, faux suede couch that smells of mold. I hate it. I bite my lip to remain silent. My kitchen barstools are carried to the basement and replaced with his chrome steel chairs, although I must admit they look much better than what I had there before. His accessories are blending well with mine.

The large master walk-in closet has been all mine for so many years. Everything is in its place, and my accessories are displayed exactly the way I like them. Hangers are all in the same direction, and everything is folded perfectly. I've made space for him, but I realize today that his daily presence in the closet is going to be messy. It seems odd to see a man's clothing hanging alongside mine.

I tend to be obsessive about organization throughout the house but especially in my—oops!—*our* closet. It's hard to walk around the house, where everything has been in its place for years, to see things coming and going in a flurry without any forethought. Whatever prior discussions we had about rearranging the house have gone out the window; nothing is going as planned. I'm getting agitated, and I remind him of our agreement about furniture placement. He agrees and puts a stop to any more moves without my input.

Okay, I think, my heart beating rapidly. *Good. He's listening. This will all be okay after today. Maybe I'm just a control freak. Maybe I should just lighten up.*

Jake and Dylan make two trips between his house and mine, bringing in more furniture and belongings with no idea of where it all will go. The garage, basement, and wine cellar begin to fill up with junk, and I become silently distraught once again.

As moving day draws to a close, I take a few quiet moments to reassess this emotional time. Each room in the house is aglow, due to Jake's love of candles. The scent of beef stew simmering in the crockpot drifts through the house, drawing everyone to the kitchen, which reminds me that this man is a wonderful cook. Julia and Zoey are helpful. Overall, things have gone well, but my nerves are still getting the best of me.

While I am deep in thought, Jake approaches me from behind, wrapping his arms lovingly around me before he heads to bed. We sway back and forth in sync as he whispers softly, "Our first night of living together. I am so happy. I love you, sweetie."

Exhausted after moving furniture all day, he goes to bed early, leaving me time to wander through the house, rearranging things at my leisure. Finally finished, I find myself smiling as I walk into the bedroom to find him settled snugly in our bed.

As I climb in next to him, I hear a tiny voice in my head, giving me cause to wonder, *Do I really know this person?* My fear of commitment runs deep. *Lighten up, Stella,* I think. *Everything's gonna be okay. You've got a great guy. He loves you, and you love him.*

I gingerly pull the covers to my shoulders, turn off my light, and curl up next to my man, trying not to wake him. I love his smell and the feel of his back against the palm of my hands and my feet rubbing against his. His soft breathing lulls me to sleep.

This is a good thing. Today turned out to be a good day.

Chapter 8
Autumn 2011

THE CASUAL DAYS OF summer have worn me out as autumn, my favorite season, makes its debut. Mother Nature does her best work this time of year, offering a season of color and cooler temperatures before slamming the Northeast with snow and frigid temperatures. But those few weeks of pumpkins, warm apple pies, and peak foliage make it all worthwhile.

It's the time of year to put the household back in order, with a revised schedule and an in-depth drawer and closet cleaning—for I am the ultimate organizer. I like predictable outcomes and order to my days. I don't handle upheaval well.

The end of summer marks another college departure, this time for my daughter, Julia. She is leaving the nest, and it's no easier or less emotional than when my son, Harris, departed for Arizona. Julia and I pack for the college road trip, transporting her life to South Carolina. I selfishly feel that it is too far away, but she has been steadfast with her decision. Clemson is her first-choice school; she has her sights set on the varsity rowing team and their strong Life Science program. Nothing is going to hold her back. As sad as I am to be so far away from Julia, I know I have to back off and get out of her way. She's been ready for this move since the first time we toured the campus. This beautiful girl of mine who has always known her power is ready to spread her wings.

We pack the car tightly with her belongings, emptying the important items from her room into her new dorm-style plastic drawers, as Riley watches with despair in his eyes. The room where Julia and Riley spent each night together, doing homework and sleeping late on weekends, is now a shell of what it once was, and Riley has no idea why.

Within days of Julia's departure, Zoey deems the entire third floor of the house and all three bedrooms officially hers. After years of being the youngest, she now single-handedly rules the roost to her liking. How sweet to finally enjoy the perks of being the youngest! But the house just isn't the same without Julia. Zoey misses her sister, and so do I. Riley is distressed; he spends his days sleeping under Julia's bed, wondering when and if his favorite person will ever return.

And so, another school year begins. The alarms are set for 6:00 a.m., reflecting a new schedule for Zoey, now a high-school freshman.

Jake and I are still working through the roommate glitches. Regardless of the snags we've encountered, I am genuinely happy to be living with him. I feel safe with him in my life; there's a sense of security that I haven't felt in a long time. We blend nicely together as friends, lovers, and partners.

This man who rang my doorbell that day is now making my kitchen dream come true with a full renovation. I am elated with the design plans. It's inspiring to have a partner who works with his hands, who molds my ideas to perfection.

As he demolishes the old tile backsplash and Formica countertops, Jake's shoulder muscles ripple through his T-shirt with each swing of the crowbar.

One week later, the granite counter is installed, transforming the kitchen into the shining jewel of the house. This is followed by the natural stone backsplash. New appliances are delivered, and the kitchen is cleaned until it sparkles. I realize his efforts are a romantic gesture, and I am all in.

After the granite crew leaves and Zoey heads out for the evening, Jake lifts me onto the counter and kisses me. With a smile he says, "This is what I wanted to do the day I walked into this house and met you for the first time."

Next on Jake's renovation agenda is the formal living room. He picks out the new wall color, a dark charcoal gray. It's a bold change, but I like it.

While the faux painting on the walls might be outdated, the furniture is classic white, given to me by my mother. Like everything passed down from a mother to a daughter, the emotional attachment to the pieces makes them priceless. The white couch and chairs are a timeless touch alongside the baby grand piano, fireplace, and gleaming hardwood floors.

I'll be out of town while the room is being painted, escaping to Naples, and leaving it to Jake to send me pictures of the progress. His texts arrive throughout my weekend away: "You won't believe how beautiful the room is, babe. Looks like a whole new house!"

Arriving back home, I step through the front door with anticipation. Natural light pours in through the sliding glass doors with the autumn foliage—at its peak—as the backdrop. The fireplace is glowing. The new wall color is perfect.

But I'm confused by the fact that the room is void of furniture, with the exception of my piano. "Where is my furniture?" I speak before thinking, realizing too late that I have muttered the territorial word *my*, and I cringe. Jake dislikes the term *my*. He prefers *ours*.

He shrugs his shoulders. "I don't like the furniture that was here. It's outdated. I'll buy you new furniture."

I ask him again, "Where is my furniture? My white couch and chairs? I love that furniture. That was my mom's furniture. Where is it?"

He replies, "Didn't you hear me? Go and buy some new furniture. Get whatever you want. It's my treat. I'm trying to renovate the things you wanted changed. Your furniture is in the attic. I didn't throw away your furniture, Stella."

He is clearly irritated with my lack of appreciation for the new paint color, and I'm irritated that he sent me texts and pictures of the project all weekend and never mentioned the fact that my furniture was being packed away in the attic.

"I never asked for new furniture, and we never discussed new furniture," I insist. "I like the furniture that was here. It fit the room nicely. I wish you had asked me first. The furniture is mine to decide about."

Oops! I've done it again, uttering the word *mine* rather than *ours*— another territorial violation.

"Nice to see you appreciate everything in *your* house," he grouses.

"I appreciate all of it, but you didn't discuss the furniture with me—just like the family room couch. You didn't broach that with me either. My leather couch went out the door the day you moved in. Now you have stripped the living room without asking me. I don't like that. Not cool."

He stares at me blankly. "Obviously, you didn't hear me. Go buy whatever furniture you want. If you want me to get your shitty, out-dated furniture from the attic, then I will."

I need to take a breather from the conversation, so I exit to my— oops, I mean *our*—bedroom to unpack and give myself time to process what I have just walked into. Conversing with myself as I unpack, I still can't make sense of it.

I am appreciative, I say to myself, but how in the hell do you just store away a woman's furniture without telling her? Why couldn't he have let me know first? I'd just assumed the room would be put back together once the paint dried. As unimportant as the situation is, it doesn't sit well with me—yet, at the same time, I don't want to make a big deal out of nothing. Is it nothing, or is it something? It's just plain confusing, to say the least.

For the next few days, every time I walk past the empty living room, a feeling of disappointment overcomes me. I don't really want new furniture.

Time passes, and it has a way of healing wounds—or perhaps we assume an unspoken indifference when things are not resolved between partners.

I'm starting to soften as I settle into our life together, although the transition has been more challenging than I had anticipated. Jake senses my resistance, and I must admit it's real. I have been a tad reluctant. I see small signs that make me wonder what his intent might or might not be. Sometimes it seems as though he likes to confuse me.

A few weeks later, still uneasy with the empty living room and no resolution in sight, I succumb to his wishes. *Perhaps some new living room furniture will lighten my mood after all,* I think.

My spirits lift as I wander from store to store, sitting on couch after couch, liking what I see. Within a few hours, I've picked out new living room furniture and am feeling a bit more appreciative of Jake's insistence that we update the room. I place the furniture order with a deposit on my credit card, calling Jake as I leave the store, to share my excitement.

I can hear the hesitation in his voice. "Oh, I didn't know you were going to do it now. I think we should wait a few months."

I'm silent for a moment. Then I say impulsively, "Just put my furniture back and stop wasting my fucking time."

My comment is met with silence.

"Hello. Are you still there?" I ask.

He responds, "Are you finished bitching at me now?"

The conversation ends with a simple click. This is our first, and hopefully the last, abrupt hang-up phone call that we'll experience as a couple. I can only hope.

Arriving home, I hear the echo of emptiness coming from the living room, creating a wary disappointment for me. Such minor things between Jake and me cause an odd sense of anxiety and result in an awkward silence between us. I'm not sure what any of it means.

I need to replenish my energy and seek some private space. Picking up Riley's hiking collar brings him to my side instantly, panting with excitement. He knows exactly what that jingle means—a hike on "Riley Hill." I'm spending more time hiking these trails lately. Climbing to the top of the hill is where the real beauty takes place. No matter how many times I come here, I pause to stand in this spot, in awe of the meadow grasses that expand for acres, swaying in the breeze.

Anchored on the horizon is a perfectly renovated antique farmhouse painted in the slightest green shade that blends perfectly into the landscape. Next to it is a red barn surrounded by ancient, sweeping oak trees that drape their shade over the roof. On the second floor of the barn, a piece of the exterior wall has been replaced with an enormous plate glass window, allowing me a glimpse into a renovated home office, complete with a stone fireplace that reaches to the ceiling and an old armchair positioned by the window, offering the lucky homeowner a stunning view that I envy each time I pass by.

Local tales claim the house and barn have been owned by a local family and passed down through many generations. They were kind enough to recently donate the surrounding acres of hiking trails to the public, offering refuge to anyone who is lucky enough to know this gem exists. This is my sanctuary, sitting under a single tree in the middle of the meadow with a 360-degree view of pure heaven on earth. I never tire of this spot that I have secretly renamed Riley Hill.

Riley runs carefree through the meadow, where the grass is so high that the tip of his tail is all I can see. He returns to my side when I give the signature whistle I created just for him. Panting, his tongue hanging out to the side, he waits to be praised for his prompt return. He's such a regal and obedient dog.

I chat with Riley as we walk the path along the way, telling him my thoughts as he trots in front of me. We both know where he is headed—straight toward his favorite apple tree. I sit in the shade of the tree, giving him time to find the perfect apple. With my approval, he eats it skillfully, using only his front teeth and avoiding the core. We rest silently together, taking the time to honor the view and the aroma of the season.

Early autumn is abundant here today. The air is so crisp that I can't help but fill my lungs to capacity with each deep breath. Leaves on their branches sway in the breeze, creating a wash of colorful hues. Every few seconds another leaf spirals softly downward to blanket the ground for the inevitable frost. In mere weeks, the hay bales will be harvested in preparation for the approaching winter. Today, I'm living for the moment in this colorful afternoon. From where I sit, you can see the Boston skyline, 20 miles away as the eagle flies. It delights me to know that, just a short distance away, my old North End city neighborhood is bustling with activity, while I rest under this tree, surrounded by the calmness of autumn, admiring the skyline from afar with Riley at my side.

Today's hike has brought forth many thoughts for contemplation. I've gone from confusion to frustration about the living room scenario, and I can't seem to make headway with it. So, I rest on my faith that Jake and I will work through it somehow.

On the final mile of our hike, I feel my chest becoming heavy once more, not because of the hill Riley and I are climbing but because of the newness of my life. My mind wanders from the past to the present in hope of finding respite in how I feel about my life today.

I do better alone, I think, as we head back to the house. It's been that way since I was a young girl, when I began retreating to my room to be alone. I knew at a young age that solitude was a virtue for me and the same rings true today. I'm not afraid to be by myself. I enjoy my own company as much as I savor being in the company of others; both have their rightful place in life.

To date, the most fulfilling relationship has been my nine-year marriage with my ex-husband, Corey. We enjoyed an equality between us, a friendship and courtship of five years before we discussed marriage. Honestly, he still is the only person I am comfortable with in my personal space. Divorces happen, and life moves on, but I never gave up on our friendship. Over the years we have become friendly once more. When I am left alone to celebrate our kids' accomplishments, is when I miss him the most.

I have a busy life managing kids, a home, and a long-standing career as an educational consultant. Most men I meet are impressed with my drive and my independence but are confused as to how they might fit into my busy life. In the past, my message to them has been so simple that they have a hard time comprehending it: There is no need to enter my life. Why not just enjoy the walk alongside each other, sharing only what we choose? Why does everything have to blend at this stage of our divorced lives?

I've grown to detest the word *blend*. To me, it means losing independence and gaining someone else's baggage from past relationships that I would prefer not to touch. Post-divorce relationships at my age come with a different set of rules regarding commitment, as far as I'm concerned. Why is there always a race toward a shared front door or the golden ring around a finger? Why not just enjoy the presence of someone special in your life without navigating toward some level of ownership?

Riley, who prides himself on his speed and agility, sees movement out of the corner of his eye. He sprints forward, breaking my thoughts and bringing me back to the moment. Pouncing with precision, he lands the fresh kill of a field mouse with just one gentle bite to its neck. Trotting proudly, he comes to sit attentively at my feet, offering me his kill. After I praise him with a loving pat on his head and give the mouse a proper burial in the stone wall, Riley leads the way with purpose, knowing that his dinner awaits him upon our return.

My worries for today remain unresolved. Nevertheless, Riley and I walk toward home with a lighter step and a warmer heart after our hike on Riley Hill.

Chapter 9
Winter Holiday 2011

ON OUR FIRST THANKSGIVING together, I wake to find my Christmas trees have been brought down from the attic and Jake is outside stringing lights on the trees. The front yard is festive with lights, enticing me to start decorating on the inside.

When he takes my white tree out of the box, Jake is surprised that it's tacky white instead of green. He teases me as I assemble the white branches to its 12-foot trunk, the top branches brushing against the ceiling.

I chuckle defensively. "Yeah, yeah, yeah. Go ahead and make fun but wait 'til you see it decorated!"

My Christmas trees are the highlight of the holiday season and a reflection of my passion for photography. The sealed box of decorations Jake has retrieved from the attic holds twenty-five years of handmade photo tree ornaments, a craft I have perfected over the years, documenting memorable moments in the life of our family. Each one is different from the others, with decorative paper stock and sequined borders surrounding each special photograph. The backs of the ornaments are personalized with names, dates, vacation spots, poems, or a list of gifts the child received from Santa that year. They are snapshots in time that are recaptured every year at Christmas, sparkling on the branches of my white tree. It's a holiday walk down memory lane.

This year I want to make sure Jake's family is included on the tree, so throughout November I secretly made photo ornaments for his side of the family. The white tree is assembled and decorated late into the evening. We dim the overhead lights, and turn on the tree lights, which shed a luminous glow over the room. Twinkling lights shine on each photograph. Jake stands with his arm around my waist, in awe, amazed at how a tacky, dusty, white tree in a box can transform into something so elegant, shining brightly by the picture window. The ornaments glisten, and large peacock feathers tucked between the branches augment with blue and gold shadows.

Jake steps closer to admire the custom ornaments. After a few moments, he stops when he finds a family picture of his own hanging from a branch. Then he discovers more ornaments as he circles the tree slowly. He sees a picture of his daughter as a young child, a fishing snapshot of his son, a vintage photograph of his parents bordered with silver sequins, and a photo of the two of us at Naples Beach, taken on his birthday weekend.

Smiling, he quietly says, "This is the most beautiful tree ever."

It is the exact reaction I am looking for. For Jake and me, this is the perfect moment to declare the beginning of the holiday season and our first Christmas together.

The highlight of the season for Jake is his annual holiday Christmas party, a tradition complete with a competitive Yankee swap, cocktails, and humorous camaraderie from his boisterous family. He takes this party as seriously as I take my Christmas trees, and we are looking forward to hosting it together this year.

This will be the first time I meet his family. I eagerly take on the hostess role and dive into planning the menu, shopping for gifts, and arranging the house for the party. Yet I'm surprised to find Jake sullen and irritated with my involvement as the party draws near. It's a definite mood change from earlier weeks, when he was excited for us to do this together.

My party planning brings me front and center to the still-empty living room that echoes every time I pass by. I've grown to resent the hollow emptiness of the room. It's been too long since the room was dismantled. A sarcastic response meets any suggestion from me to complete the room before the holidays. So, I avoid the conversation altogether, because he's made it clear that this bare space doesn't bother him. My distress over it seems to bother him even less.

As the holidays approach, Jake eventually responds to my request by filling the empty living room with eighteen metal folding chairs, placing them in a large circle. Despite our disagreement, it seems that he is more determined than ever to leave the room impersonal and an embarrassment to me.

It's no surprise when he continues the discussion via text, a technique he began using shortly after he moved in. Despite the fact that I'm in the next room, close enough to talk face to face, he sends me a text instead, informing me that my involvement in his family party is no longer needed. Jokingly, I blurt out loud enough for him to hear in the adjoining room, "Have I been fired from my own party?" My comment is confirmed with a texted thumbs-up emoji.

Just like that, the holiday celebration takes a turn in the wrong direction, breathing new life into territorial discord between us. His dismissive texts make me cringe with their abrupt and sometimes callous messages. The vulgarity that raised a red flag at the beginning of our relationship still bothers me.

A day before the family party, the awkward moments have subsided somewhat, with both of us choosing not to exchange contentious remarks. I tidy up the house, make the party appetizers, and straighten the decorations. I place as many candles and holiday decorations on the baby grand piano as I can, trying to make up for the folding chairs, but nothing seems to camouflage the emptiness of the room. No matter how I decorate it, the room looks like an old-fashioned funeral parlor.

His daughter's arrival from Chicago brightens up the household, because no one brings more Christmas cheer than Natalie does. Natalie and Dylan join my family tradition of decorating gingerbread houses, creating merriment for this group who is struggling to settle into a shared house. The kitchen is full of laughter. Bags of candy are spread across the island. Various colors of homemade frosting cover our fingers and our lips.

When we leave difficulties behind and just enjoy the happy mess in front of us, the house becomes a home, and the mood, once protective, turns jubilant. We make up gingerbread contest rules as we go, spying on one another's creations and trying to steal ideas. It's one of the happier memories of this marriage that I will always remember.

Jake's family party serves as the official reveal of the newly renovated kitchen. I must say that the room is stunning, and, despite our holiday discord, we are both excited for the night ahead.

The guests are appointed to judge the gingerbread houses, which serve as the holiday centerpiece on the granite countertop. We each campaign for votes, showing off our gingerbread creations. As the cocktails and high spirits continue, Natalie is deemed the winner. From that day forward, gingerbread houses become a friendly competitive bond that Natalie and I share. I still think of her every time I see one.

Jake is busy making his guests the holiday-themed French and eggnog martinis we had conjured up for the party menu. The Christmas trees gleam with holiday cheer throughout the house. The three fireplaces are crackling, and Christmas cards decorate the mantels. Riley, wearing his Christmas bandana, follows the guests, waiting patiently for morsels of food to be dropped onto the floor. It's Christmas overload in our house, and it's exactly the way we like it.

Jake relies on me as the party takes shape. I see it as a good sign, and, quite honestly, I am happy to help, putting the stress of the past few weeks behind us. I begin setting up the buffet as the food is delivered, a menu I had spent a lot of time planning before Jake relieved me of my hostess duties. As I uncover the buffet dishes, I realize the restaurant has delivered the wrong food.

At that moment, noticing the look of confusion on my face, Jake approaches me, putting his arm around my waist. Speaking quietly, he says, "I changed the items on the menu back to what Natalie and I like to serve."

I stand still for a moment in silence, with my back to the guests. It's hard to take up an issue with your significant other when his family is celebrating all around. Initially, I am upset with his daughter's interference, but then, in mere moments, I realize that she most likely had nothing to do with it. She probably doesn't even know I planned a menu. My silent, stiff reaction doesn't seem to affect Jake. He kisses me on the cheek and casually moves away from me to show off the house to his family, complimenting my taste in decorating.

As I prepare the food, I can't help but think that this incident is similar to the living room furniture issue, wherein I find the offense to be subtle and hard to detect. Yet it stings just enough to hurt, leaving me to wonder once more whether this is something or nothing. I focus on remaining composed as my second martini kicks in, putting me at ease for the remainder of the evening.

Despite the interference with the menu, I adore his family. They are a welcoming, friendly, and warmhearted bunch. At the end of the night, his family and I part with hugs and Christmas wishes. With the house quiet, Jake hugs me, and we laugh as we recall the fun evening. Then he retires to bed, leaving me to clean up.

I am still ripe from my two martinis, and when he announces he is turning in for the night I want nothing more than to spout off at him. But I don't. I just walk through the quiet house, picking up trash and saying all the things to Riley that I want to say to Jake.

The next morning, as we are resting on the couch and eating party leftovers, I make a failed attempt to talk to Jake. "Why did you change the food I ordered?" I'm looking for resolution, thinking we can find a better way to plan for next year. But I can't get him to focus on the topic.

"Why the hell do you have to bring that up? No one is going to tell me how to host my own family party," he says.

I respond, "I thought we had originally agreed to host it as a couple. I wasn't trying to tell you what to do."

"You did host. You were there, weren't you?"

"Geez," I mutter under my breath as I walk away.

New Year's Eve is off to a quiet start, just the way we planned. Much to my surprise, I come home to find my mother's furniture back in its rightful place. I take it as a positive sign. I'm relieved to put the living room dilemma behind us.

Jake and I enjoy steamed lobster by candlelight, as we plan to settle in for a quiet New Year's Eve at home, in our pajamas. I am pleasantly surprised when Zoey ends up with us on this festive night, creating a long overdue opportunity for Jake and Zoey to spend time together. Jake bakes all night with her. They deep-fry pastries and make peanut butter cookies, cream cheese brownies, and fried pickles.

I can see Zoey beginning to smile in his presence. The two of them cook side by side as I watch—sitting on a stool, drinking wine, sampling their creations, taking in the sight of my beautiful new kitchen, and watching two people I love getting to know each other.

We spend the winter season nestling through the blizzards and record cold temperatures, staying warm in front of the roaring fires that Jake likes to build. We resort to fireside weekend dates that suit us both fine and entice me to fall asleep wrapped in his arms while watching movies.

Snowstorms, once a huge burden on me, cause me no worry now, with Jake in my life. He can't contain his excitement when snow is forecast. To him, it's a major event. He arrives home with bags of groceries for a hearty winter meal and then snowplows the front and back driveway to perfection. He treats snowplowing like a sport, with Riley following behind, chomping on the snow flying out the chute. This man melts my heart when he creates plowed snow mazes throughout the front yard and backyard for Riley.

With each snowstorm, Jake designs new paths to connect to the older paths, complete with twists and turns and mini mountains. Riley loves to explore the expansive obstacle course that eventually leads him from the backyard to our front door with tail wagging and snow dripping from his ears.

Jake brings the quads home from work at the mere mention of a snowstorm, so we can four-wheel through the streets during a snow emergency, all of us dressed in ski gear, helmets, and goggles. For the first time in many years, the freezing cold is fun again.

We are growing closer to each other, moving past misgivings that we bury under present love. We've worked hard to overcome our differences and have created a nice life together. Our conversations are easy, and our rapport is fluid, with the momentum bringing us to new heights as a couple. His humor makes me laugh every day. I am more at ease with the progression of our relationship now, happy I'm with someone who means so much to me. The year 2012 is off to a great start.

Chapter 10
Spring 2012

AS USUAL, JAKE IS keeping things fresh; he's always on the move. With just a two-day notice, we are on a flight from Boston to Naples, taking Dylan along for the ride. As soon as we're seated on the airplane, I pop my medication to fight off the nausea of flying, a burden I've dealt with for years.

"Ya know you're supposed to take that two hours before you fly, right?" Jake says with a smile.

"Too late now," I say.

We have a good laugh, and no sooner do I shut my eyes that it seems Jake is nudging me awake for our landing. But this time I'm groggier than usual. He escorts me through the airport, making fun of my delirious state of mind, and gets me safely into the passenger seat of the rental car, where I fall asleep again.

When we arrive at the condo, he unpacks and changes for the beach sunset as I lie on the bed, watching him through my sleepy eyes.

Jake pulls on my arm, coaxing me to join him on the beach. "Come on, honey. I really want to go to the beach for the sunset."

I smile, playfully pushing him away as I beg for just a few more minutes of sleep. I wake an hour later to find him standing over me when I pry open my eyes. The meds have maintained their grip on me.

He's a bit irritated but laughing as he nudges me for the second time today. "Really? You missed such a great sunset. You really missed it, Stella!"

He brushes by the bed, just within my reach. I catch hold of the back of his bathing suit to expose his white buttocks. "There will be plenty more of those to watch together. I'm sorry. The nausea meds really knock me out."

We both laugh as he grabs my wrists, pulling me to a standing position. He navigates me by my shoulders and steers us into the shower. The hot water invigorates me. He scrubs my scalp with shampoo, clearing my head back to normalcy. Within an hour, I'm sitting at the oceanside bar, sipping a martini with my best friend, Jake.

I'm finally alert and flirting with my boyfriend, feeling so happy that I hadn't stopped him from planning this weekend. He snaps a selfie of the two of us and posts the picture of the happy couple on social media. Life is good. Being in love makes it even better.

Jake and I spend the next day watching Dylan surf and swim in the ocean, while we relax under the beach umbrella. Later in the afternoon, I sit twenty floors up on the condo's lanai, looking down at the spot where we spent the day in the sand. The sunscreen glistens on my skin, and the last remaining particles of sand are stuck to my shoulders. I swivel gently back and forth in the high-top chair, enjoying a glass of wine and a full plate of cheese and crackers all to myself. I feel content to be in this moment. Nothing could keep me from this view, not even Jake's naked body trying to entice me into the shower with him.

From where I sit, the ocean looks larger than life, spreading out before my eyes for eternity. It makes me realize it is far more powerful, beautiful, and forbidding than any other form of nature. I fear the ocean, am compelled to be near it, and find myself mesmerized by its power.

The sun casts a glow of transparency over the water, making it possible to see schools of fish and dolphins swimming under the surface. If the swimmers only knew how close some of them were! The sound of the waves brings a sense of calm to the beautiful view. This is relaxation and appreciation at its best.

I'm uninhibited, sitting there with not a care in the world, lost in the moment, casually examining my tanned toes and sunburnt knees. Jake walks toward me, freshly showered and bare chested. I inhale the scent of his cologne and clean skin, as he wraps his arms around me from behind. Both of us stare out into the ocean, as I chatter away.

"Year after year I sit here, and each time the view astonishes me, as if it's the first time," I say quietly.

As I'm speaking, he swivels my chair around to face him. Reaching out, he places his hands on my thighs, as I continue talking about our day at the beach.

He looks at me and starts laughing. "Can you just be quiet for a minute?"

He gazes into my eyes, but my mouth is full of cheese and crackers. I sense something emotional, but I don't know whether it's good or bad news. He continues to look at me, as I take a large sip of wine to wash down the cheese and crackers. I can feel his nervousness. Our eyes lock together as he kisses me.

Taking a small step backward, he says to me, "The day I met you was the best day of my life. I love and trust you more than anyone I've ever known, and I want to spend the rest of my life with you." He drops to one knee and pulls out a small box, opening it to show a diamond ring. "Will you please marry me? I will make you the happiest woman on earth. I promise."

I am shocked and dumbfounded. We have not had a conversation about marriage, but I've certainly had enough dialog with myself. I'm not sure how long I pause before answering; I am trying to process my initial panic, which is mixed with flattery and happiness.

I can see he is becoming nervous, so I quickly blurt out, "Yes, an engagement is nice, but a long one, okay?"

He smiles at me, sealing it with a passionate kiss. Thoughts rush through my mind in a matter of seconds. *So now I've got the shared front door and the ring around my finger?*

My heart responds to my head: Things have been going so well! We've come so far, and he makes me happy. Life is easy and fun with him in it. I love him.

My head doesn't agree; more thoughts ramble in my mind. *What about those conversations with Riley about independence and post-divorce baggage?*

Jake pops champagne, and we watch our first sunset as an engaged couple.

Moments later, we share the news with Dylan, who responds with a cheery handshake for his dad and a bear hug for me. We finish the bottle of champagne, smiling ear to ear, not wanting this special moment to end.

He tells me of the proposal he had planned the night before, to take place on the beach at sunset. Through his laughter, he says, "Honey, you slept through my proposal! I had everything ready down at the beach last night, with a blanket and champagne, but you were snoring in bed!"

My mouth drops open in disbelief. "I had no clue!"

The sun, a bright orange ball of fire this evening, sinks slowly into the ocean, leaving the sky glowing with happiness. I feel just a tiny bit of apprehension, which I manage to swallow in honor of the moment.

Arriving home to Larington, we dive into finishing the house. I become more settled with the idea of our engagement. We turn the corner on our commitment to each other, clearing the air of past grievances and being proactive about others. While Zoey is still not accepting of Jake, over time our kids have slowly become tolerant of each other.

During Jake's business travels, we text each other constantly, sending romantic and silly thoughts. He clearly misses me and our nights together when he's away. Every phone call ends with "I love you." Every text is rife with heart emojis. Laughter embraces our house. We are true partners, lovers, and a future married couple. One season blends into the next, our foundation strong and our future solid.

Chapter 11
Spring 2013

OUR YEAR-LONG ENGAGEMENT eventually warms my thoughts on marriage. We have blended seamlessly, despite my initial apprehension. With the ocean waves lapping on shore, both of us in bare feet, with bright sunshine overhead and blessed smiles on our faces, one year after he proposed, we elope. It's the perfect Naples beach day to be married.

We spend the morning of our wedding day beachside, soaking up the sun, diving into the ocean waves, and lunching poolside. The laughs and the jokes between us go on all day long. We are giddy with anticipation of our nuptials, which are to take place in just a few hours.

I'm in an ocean-blue halter maxi dress, Jake in a Tommy Bahama shirt and shorts. We share a glass of wine while we wait—the sun's position will determine the timing of our unconventional wedding procession down the boardwalk. Jake carries a bottle of wine and two glasses. I hold in one hand a small gardenia bouquet, its stems wrapped in satin ribbon, and carry my stiletto shoes in the other.

Barefoot, we meet the justice of the peace at the shore and turn to face each other, eager to say our vows at the exact spot where we sunbathed on Jake's birthday weekend.

Our elopement is a private affair, with only my mother, a hired photographer, and random walkers on the beach as our witnesses. We want an intimate, yet casual, ceremony with no guests, not even our kids. It's just the two of us, followed with a quick honeymoon weekend at the beach.

Little children still in their bathing suits giggle, admiring us from afar. Lovers on a sunset walk pause briefly, smiling at the romance of a beach wedding for only two. We recite our vows and exchange rings with tears of happiness brimming in our eyes. The justice of the peace proclaims us husband and wife, and we seal her pronouncement with a passionate kiss, as the sun descends gracefully, making its way to a pivotal sunset in my life.

The photographer works quickly to capture our joy, posing us on the shore as the sun sinks lower. Just moments after the ceremony, a large, spectacular cloud appears overhead, making for an extraordinary photograph.

Standing together at the ocean's shore, me still holding my bouquet, we pose as the storm cloud expands, engulfing the sun's rays, creating a sudden darkness and emptying the beach with its threat of rain—leaving only us under the cloud. It is a breathtaking contrast of sun and storm appearing before our eyes, a photographer's dream come true.

After the ceremony, just the two of us holding hands, we walk the beach to a romantic dinner for two at the Ritz-Carlton. As our favorite server greets us, she leads us to a reserved dining couch tucked away in a quiet corner of the room, where we have our own private view of the ocean.

Drinking wine and sitting romantically close, we dine casually on tapas, starting off with a variety of cheeses, prosciutto, and figs. Next come samplings of fresh lobster with drawn butter, ahi tuna, zucchini fritters, and finally a customized dessert sampling of warm bread pudding, crème brûlée, and berries drizzled with melted dark chocolate. Those seated near us send congratulatory greetings, winks, and smiles.

It is a private, romantic wedding reception for two, exactly the way we want it to be.

Over dinner, Jake and I review the moments of our ceremony. We feel so fortunate that the photographer and his lens were able to capture the symbolic contrast between sun and storm. I have no idea at the time that the storm cloud hovering as we were proclaimed husband and wife should be heeded as a warning.

Only our children were privy to our wedding plans, and they kept our secret well. Just three days after we eloped, we board a flight back to Boston as newlyweds, both of us still high on the romance of our wedding weekend. Just before the wheels lift from the runway, we announce our marriage on social media, accompanied by a photograph of us, the happy couple, standing ankle deep in the ocean, flowers in hand, and our joyous faces smiling under a spectacular storm cloud.

The first few honeymoon months that follow are blissful. I enjoy being married to this man, even though I did at first shy away from a commitment with him. Our children are somewhat supportive, or at least tolerant of the newly formed union. No relationship is ever perfect, but our marriage is off to a good start and good intentions.

Pillow talk is the highlight of our bedtime ritual. "No drama. No outsiders. No lies. It's us and our kids. We are a family. Honesty trumps everything."

Chapter 12
Early Fall 2013

WE HAVE LONG BEEN anticipating Julia's visit from South Carolina. I can't wait to see her smiling face again. It will be even more exciting for Riley to see his favorite human. Julia's laughter lights up the house as usual, and Riley doesn't let her out of his sight. I love it when my kids return home to visit, but their departure still knocks the wind out of me. Soon after Julia's weekend visit, Jake approaches me and accuses Julia of stealing from our master bedroom closet.

I respond with confusion to the accusation: "My kids are in my room all the time."

He doesn't like my answer and proceeds to show me a picture of Julia in my closet, borrowing some of my clothes, although he refers to it as "stealing."

I laugh at the absurdity. "Jake, my girls and I have been stealing clothes out of one another's closets for years! How did you get this picture of Julia?"

Seeking my approval, he says, "I keep this family safe," and he shows me the tiny battery-operated camera he had hidden in my closet.

"What are you doing? Are you secretly monitoring us in our own home? Do you monitor me in my own closet? How dare you!" I scream.

"Where else do you use this camera? Don't you *ever* use another hidden camera in this house! We don't spy on one another here!"

He apologizes profusely, handing me the camera. "Here, take it. I'm sorry. It was wrong of me. I love Julia. I wasn't spying. I set up the hidden camera in case we got robbed."

I have no words left to say.

The hidden camera sheds a light onto the paranoid shift I have observed in his behavior lately. Recently he has insinuated that he thinks someone is stealing from him or is out to betray him. Since learning of the hidden camera, I wonder if there might be additional surveillance elsewhere. I scour the house, finding nothing. My thoughts take me a bit deeper. I wonder whether he would be bold enough to reconnect the security cameras I disconnected shortly after he had them installed a few months back. Reconnecting them would enable him to use his cell phone to monitor us from anywhere—the exact reason I disconnected them. I hated those cameras, and my kids were furious with me for allowing them to be installed. Now, for the first time, I feel a bit of paranoia myself, wondering whether someone is watching.

My probing questions about his surveillance anger him, setting off a lot of swearing aimed at me. The term *fuck off* is being thrown my way more frequently, especially when I question him about possible surveillance of the house. It becomes difficult to keep him on topic. He digs deep into insults and accusations concerning my loyalty to our marriage, claiming I don't trust him. His twisted words do not fool me. It is he who does not trust—to the point where he believes hidden cameras are warranted.

Chapter 13
The Pool, Early Spring 2013

AT THE END OF a long day, Jake arrives home walking tall, filled with excitement. Taking me by the hand and pulling me into the kitchen, he unrolls a set of plans for a backyard pool. I'm giddy with excitement.

"You've wanted a pool for so long. Is this what you like?" he asks. "You can pick out all the stone and tile, and I'll do the excavation and installation."

I'm ecstatic. In my mind, I see a beautifully landscaped backyard with burgers on the grill and kids splashing in the pool. There I am, casually sipping a Chardonnay on a beautiful afternoon, with my feet dangling in the water.

"Finally, a pool!" I say to Jake as I wrap my arms around his neck. I stand on my tiptoes to kiss his cheek as he continues, talking excitedly about the plans. And then comes the question.

"If you front the initial $10,000 out of your account, then I will do the rest out of mine." Finances are an awkward topic for us to discuss due to my refusal to blend finances when we married.

"Sure, I'll front the $10,000, but you are responsible for the rest, including outdoor furniture," I say.

He seals the agreement with a definitive "yes" and a hug.

A few weeks later, early on a Sunday morning, the excavator arrives to begin the project. We watch with excitement as the backhoe tears the emerging spring grass up by its roots, exposing the earth beneath and establishing the hole that will soon be our pool. Watching the blade tear apart the irrigation pipes make me cringe. I remind myself that I'm married to an experienced contractor. He has secured the best people and has the best connections for materials. *All is well*, I think convincingly to myself. *Jake has my back. He'll make this work out okay.*

A few hours into the excavation, the outline of a pool begins to emerge from the dirt. Knowing I love excavators, Jake invites me into the cab to give me a quick lesson on operating the lift. He videos me as I maneuver the levers in the cab, laughing as I dig deep into the earth and transfer the load to a large dirt pile.

"This is going to be so awesome!" I say to Jake as I exit the cab.

After the initial stage of the project, we hit a delay, with no explanation from Jake. This makes me nervous. Jake's time management on projects is not always great. The unfinished projects he has abandoned in the house are adding up, and I'm hoping this won't be the case with the backyard. I get a bit nervous when the excavator doesn't move for days.

As if he's reading my mind, I receive a text from Jake the next day while I'm at work, informing me he's finishing up the excavation and giving me reason to rush home early to see the progress.

Pulling into the driveway at the end of the day, I'm so excited that I head directly to the backyard for the official viewing of the pool. I look up to the sky. I stare out at the beautiful woods that frame our yard, but my gaze keeps going back to the pool. I walk around the pool a few times to take it all in, and then I walk carefully through the dirt in my high heels and into the house, where Jake is preparing meatballs in the crockpot.

I say the only thing that comes to mind: "What the fuck is that out there?"

"It's a pool."

"It's a blow-up pool!" I try to keep things to an angry hush. "It is nothing but a huge raft! Why is that out there? Where is the pool? How do you even fill it up? That is not staying here! You need to get rid of that! What the hell is going on?"

He listens silently for a few minutes, as he keeps busy preparing the meatballs. Then he looks at me calmly and says, "We're going to keep this pool for the summer. I'll install the real pool in the fall."

I am becoming more furious with every passing minute. I am so angry that I'm stuttering. "W-w-w-w-what are you t-t-t-t-talking about! *The fall?* We both agreed on the timeline when you dug up the backyard, tore out the irrigation, and made a mess! Is this how you spent the $10,000 I invested in this project? By purchasing a blow-up pool? What are you thinking? It's like three fucking feet deep! You can't even swim in it! No, this is not going to be the pool for the summer! This is a million-plus-dollar neighborhood! We don't have blow-up pools in our backyards here!"

He calmly replies, with a sarcastic smile, "Yes, dear, we do. We are going to have a blow-up pool in this yard—in this fucking neighborhood."

"Why are you doing the excavation now, instead of the contractor? Did you screw the guy by not paying him? Is that the reason for the delay this week? What the hell, Jake!"

I walk away in disbelief. By the time I make it to the hallway, my heels are off and I'm undressing as I walk toward the bedroom. All I want is to get into my pajamas. It's five in the afternoon, and I just want to go to bed. Retreating to the bathroom, I once again wish for a lock on the door. I sit on the side of the tub, looking out the picture window and realizing I might have just thrown away $10,000 by putting the project and the check into my husband's hands.

My nerves are rattled, and I'm feeling such a letdown over this. The entire yard is torn up. The windows are filthy from construction dust blowing through the yard, and there in the middle of my beautiful backyard is a supersized, bright-yellow raft, surrounded by gravel and mud, waiting to be filled with 3 feet of water. This used to be a beautiful backyard, even if it didn't have a pool. Now it hurts me to look out my window. Clearly there will be no summer fun in our backyard this year, unless we want to choke on dust and be covered in dirt.

Zoey opens my bathroom door, having just arrived home from school for the day. She stands there looking at me, dumbfounded. She points to the bathroom window. "Are you kidding me? What the hell is that out there?"

I just look at her, wanting to cry, but all I can do is laugh in disbelief. "It's the pool you wanted, Zoey."

She glares at me with a sarcastic grin.

"Trust me. That pool will not be staying in this backyard."

Zoey smiles. "I'll keep that crappy pool, if you get rid of him instead."

She sits down next to me and tells me about her day, trying to take my mind off the stress. I don't like Zoey to see me upset, so I try to make light of things. She responds in kind, joking without judging me. My kids and I share a love of sarcasm, often using it as our mode of communication.

As she exits the bathroom, she smiles, gives me a double thumbs-up signal, and sarcastically says, "Hey, come on up to my room. The view of the backyard is even better from up there."

She shoots me a wink, as she closes the door behind her. I scurry up to her room, where we sit until dark. It's safe up here. Jake won't cross the threshold of Zoey's room without advanced notice and permission. She lies on her bed doing homework, and I pace the floor, looking out into the backyard from hell.

Zoey continues to crack jokes, mostly aimed at the pool. Eventually, we sneak out the front door, hop into her car, and head out for dinner. We drive away from the house quietly, like bandits, hoping to go unnoticed.

A week goes by in silence. There's no way to mistake my anger about the pool. Seething is too calm a word to express what I feel inside. Our conversations about the project never included an inflatable pool—that much I know. I have no idea what he stands to gain from this, other than he might have spent the $10,000 on something else.

Every now and then, in passing, I enter a room and say to him, "You need to get rid of the pool. This is not what we agreed on. Get rid of the pool."

He listens and walks off without answering. Each day that passes, I become more anxious; I have no idea how this is going to be resolved. I ask him to show me proof of the $10,000 I gave him to begin the pool project. He does not respond.

Saturday morning arrives, the beginning of the weekend, and Jake is back in the kitchen cooking.

I walk through the kitchen and repeat myself, "Jake, get rid of that damn raft this weekend."

I guess that is his breaking point—and mine too. He looks up from his cooking and says, "If you want that pool gone, then get your fat ass out there and get rid of it yourself. As far as I'm concerned, I'm going to fill up that pool with water and float in it all fuckin' summer."

I stare through him and respond simply, "Okay."

With that said, Jake starts laughing. "I can't wait to see this! This is gonna be fun. To watch you act like a retard out there."

I have no real plan on how to get rid of the raft, but I'm angry enough to find a way. I walk out to the backyard, and, for the first time, I touch the pool. It's been inflated, but it's still empty of water. I try to open the air plugs, but they're so big and strong that I can't pry them open with my bare hands. The rubber material is so thick that it could survive for weeks at sea.

I head to the garage, searching for something to open the plugs. I pull a large pair of pliers out of Jake's toolbox, certain these will do the trick. Heading back to my mission, I come around the corner to find him sitting on the patio, watching me.

"Great. He's got a front-row seat," I mumble under my breath. "Now he's going to watch and taunt me the entire time."

As I try to open the plugs with the pliers, Jake starts laughing loudly.

"How's that workin' for ya, retard!"

After a few more tries, I give up on the pliers. A second trip into the garage yields me a pointed chisel that is strong and sharp enough to do the job.

Jake's laughter stops, as I lift my arms overhead, swinging down in full force. I feel the pointed edge penetrate the rubber, causing a *hisssssss* as the air escapes—but the leak is so small that it is easily patchable and will take weeks for the pool to deflate. It's going to take more than a single puncture. I go back to the garage and find a boxcutter.

Threats replace his heckling. "Oh, how the police are going to love this story. I hope you're ready to pay for another pool, because I'll order it today while you sit in jail. Should I call 911 now or wait until you're finished with your tantrum?"

Pretend he's not there, I think, as I continue my mission of destruction. I walk to one end of the pool and jam the boxcutter into the raft. This time I create a large 6-inch slit rather than just a hole. It takes a lot of strength to get through this material, even more to make a slit. It is so thick that it hurts my wrists just to penetrate it.

Jake walks into the house while I make eight more long slices on all four sides of the pool and then more 2-foot slices in a crisscross pattern on the bottom of the raft, just for good measure. When I'm finished, I walk past him through the kitchen, mumbling only one statement as I pass him, "Good luck filling it up with water now, asshole."

He responds without blinking, "It's a good thing I spent that ten thousand on my kids, because you'll never see it again."

Once the weekend is behind us, I try to put this ordeal to rest in my mind. The only thing left to dispose of is the carcass of the dead pool. It's too big and heavy to drag out to the trash. It will take a few men and a truck to dispose of it. Hoping he's come to his senses, I leave for work, expecting to come home to find the mess gone. But Jake has a different plan.

When I come home, I find him out in the backyard with the tattered pool spread out neatly on the ground. By the odor, I can tell he's using some kind of glue. As I move closer, I see him gluing the slits and punctures back together. He refuses to look at me as I approach.

"Are you kidding me?" I ask sadly.

He remains bent over, gluing more sections, saying over his shoulder, "You popped my pool, you crazy bitch."

In disbelief, I turn and walk back into the house.

The next morning, I hear activity out back. Clearly the glue has dried, because I see a water truck pulling into the driveway. I always wanted a pool, but now all I want is to put the loam back, grow the grass over this mess, and stop the fighting between us. The sound of the large hose being pulled from the belly of the water truck interrupts my thoughts.

Watching the water pour into the pool, I think, *I can't believe he's doing this.* Jake and his friend stand downhill, watching it fill with water. Peeking out the window, I can see the smile on Jake's face, a look of victory, while mine shows only exasperation from behind the window's curtain.

As the truck pulls out of sight, I see the water settling in, sparkling in the pool. I think, *Well, at least it looks a tiny bit better with water in it.* And then, without notice, my wish comes true. Within seconds, the pool splits into pieces, and the water comes rushing out all at once, heading downstream in a mini tidal wave, heading straight toward Jake and his friend.

I had no idea a small body of water could move with such velocity. The strength of the water current and the speed at which it travels amazes me. It happens so fast that it is over before I can finish my first gasp. Jake and his friend, drenched, run aside to avoid getting washed away with the water pressure. The water continues to rush toward the bottom of the driveway, taking the grill and bicycles in its wake. It flows into our neighbor's yard and lifts all their children's toys into its current.

The pool, now completely flat, resembles something in the aftermath of a flood. Bicycles and toys are flipped over, and the raft is ripped to shreds. The water pressure did a far better job of destroying the pool than I did.

A few days after the tidal wave, we slowly begin to speak to each other again. It's not because we have found some magical resolution. It is just too hard to stay silent all the time while living together under one roof.

Days later, the doorbell rings. An older woman stands before me. She looks as if she's heading out for a hike in the deep woods, her outfit complete with green cargo pants tucked into a pair of tall rain boots and a floppy hat. She's carrying a clipboard. It's never a good thing when you answer the door to find someone standing before you with a clipboard.

She introduces herself. "Hi, I'm Gloria Higgins from Larington Conservation. I'm here to inspect your property for the pool permit you applied for last week. But I see you had an old plan filed with the town a few years ago that included a pool, which we already approved. That plan is due to expire, but if I could look at your backyard, and if it passes my inspection, we can extend the existing permit instead of filing for a new one."

I stand before her, frozen in panic, as I envision her reaction to the backyard mess. My mind is racing. *Wait, he told me the permit had already been issued, and now this inspector says otherwise.* Furthermore, she wants to view my backyard that now looks like a war zone. *A flood, an excavator, and split pool that Jake has, to date, refused to remove—and all done without a permit?* My blood boils.

The yard looks nothing like it did a few years ago when Conservation last inspected it. The lawn furniture is piled up against the house. The beautiful green grass that once sloped gracefully into the woods is now a mudslide. There's a half-finished stone wall that I assume also has not been granted a permit, as required by the town bylaws. Not only does the yard look like a bomb has gone off,

Jake has mowed down parts of our property that I am certain are protected conservation land.

"Today is not a good day," I say. "I'm late for an appointment. Perhaps we can schedule this for next week, when I have more time."

"No worries, I can just check the backyard. You don't need to be present for the inspection. It will only take a few minutes."

I have no choice but to let her go out back to inspect. As I escort her to the backyard, her mouth drops open in astonishment, as she looks around at the disaster zone. Her gaze moves from the 3-foot-deep hole in the ground to the remains of the raft, the mowed-down conservation land, and the half-finished stone wall. Unbeknownst to me, all of it was done without an active permit.

Her first question to me comes as expected. "Is that a blow-up pool?"

All I can do is nod my head in agreement, saying with hesitation, "It *was* a blow-up pool."

She stares at me blankly, expecting the story to continue, but I say nothing more. I raise my eyebrows and shrug my shoulders, my hands thrust deeply into the pockets of my jeans.

She looks around a bit longer. Finally, I break the awkward silence. "It's a lot to take in." There's no need to try to talk my way out of this one. There are no words to explain any of it in an authentic, comprehensive manner, because I, myself, haven't a clue how this has happened. It seems the bizarre incidents are becoming more outlandish as my marriage progresses.

Within minutes, I've been stripped of my old permit and told that I'll be answering to the Conservation Committee at the next public town meeting. With my nerves rattled, I escort her, taking the walk of shame, to her car that is parked in front of the house. She drives away slowly, looking at me with a cold, dead stare, as she leaves with my permit in her hands.

Anyone who lives in this town knows the one department you don't ever want to defy is the Conservation Committee. Two weeks later, I'm seated at a Conservation meeting with Jake's attorney, who is now my attorney. I've made it clear to Jake that he is banned from attending this meeting. Given my fury aimed at him, the last person I want present for my public lynching is him.

While waiting for my turn to be slaughtered, I wonder how I got here. Why did I let him put the permit application in my name? Why would he start without a permit? He's in the construction business, for Pete's sake. I can't oversee everything. I just wanted a small pool and a quiet life, yet I seem to be living in increasingly more stress, for one reason or another.

Before I come to any conclusion, my name is called, and I'm standing before the committee and being questioned by the members of the board. I'm given a list of restrictions and instructions and, ultimately, numerous fines, all agreed to unanimously with a definitive "aye" from each board member. The evening is finished off with a harsh public scolding. The seriousness of the committee is beginning to irritate me, and I'm trying hard to stay focused. It is seven-thirty in the evening at the end of a long workday, and I am tired. At this point, I don't really care how much they fine me. I just want to leave this room as soon as possible, so I agree to all their stipulations to expedite the end of my time before the committee.

Finally, free to go, I can't wait to get home and go to bed.

A few days later, I receive an email from Jake showing confirmation that he has sent an email to each individual Conservation Committee member, notifying them that he has researched their home addresses and they should expect a visit from him.

After reading this, I hang my head so low that my forehead rests on my desk. At that moment, Jake walks into my office with a proud smile, asking my thoughts on his email.

I slowly lift my head and say, "I want a divorce."

He laughs, thinking it's a joke, and walks out of the room.

The next morning, I receive the first of many phone calls from the Conservation Committee, informing me that the threatening email each committee member has received from my husband has been forwarded to the town's attorney. They have voted unanimously that Jake is to be banned from the home property for all future inspections.

I have no response, because I agree with them. Without my knowledge, I have become public enemy number one of the Conservation Committee, and my husband is the person who has caused it.

I have reached my limit with this entire mess—but a few days later, I find on my desk an order confirmation for the real pool to be installed. I don't say a word. I don't want to jinx it. I just file the confirmation away and hope it will happen as he said it would. Actually, what I really want is to return the property to its former condition. My husband vehemently rejects my suggestion once again.

"I'm going to make it up to you," he insists.

Chapter 14
The Pool, Summer 2013

THE POOL PERMIT IS finally reissued, with too many restrictions to list, and I've been added to Conservation's watch list. Added to my bill are new engineering costs, fees for new plans to be drawn up, fines for cutting down plantings on Conservation land and, of course, the attorney's fees for representing me at the town meeting.

The excavation begins again. This time I make sure the excavation goes deep enough to make way for a real pool, yet I still have reservations about this project. Something is not right about the whole thing. I wanted a pool company to perform the work, but instead Jake hires unskilled labor he found on Craigslist to do the plumbing and electrical work. It only angers him more when I voice my concerns. I keep my head down, hoping the entire mess will be finished soon.

I know nothing about pool installation, but it seems logical to me that there should be more of an engineering approach than this process of digging without leveling.

Once the preconstructed pool is secured in the ground, Jake and I take a celebratory walk to the deep end and back. Our eyes don't meet, and we avoid talking. At this point, silence seems to be the best remedy. I believe he is just as exhausted by this endeavor as I am. Neither of us wants to discuss it. *If only I could turn back time,* I think.

As we sit on the pool steps, myriad thoughts run through my head—and I assume his too. We speak no words, as we sit surrounded by mounds of dirt in my once-beautiful backyard sanctuary.

As grateful as I am to have the pool in the ground, I look around and suspect this backyard might not be put back together by winter, if ever.

Within days, the water truck returns, this time to fill the real pool. The hose is inserted, and water pours in until the pool is nearly full. For the first time, I'm excited about something related to this damn pool. Once it's filled, I step outside to inspect the water level. Walking gingerly in my bare feet over mud and gravel, I find the water in the shallow end spilling over the edge onto the muddy ground, while the deep end is over a foot too shallow. It dawns on me: *Oh, my gosh—the pool isn't level!*

I look up at the sky and around the yard at the same mess I've been staring at for far too long. I cannot believe my eyes. I have no words.

After this, I try to insist we use a pool company to fix the leveling problem. Instead, my husband purchases a handheld hydraulic lift, the same kind used to change a truck tire. I can't imagine that raising a pool just a few inches, shoveling dirt into a hole, and then placing the weight of a pool on the dirt is going to solve the leveling dilemma. I beg him to stop, suggesting again that he call a pool company to fix it or—even better—pull out the pool and stop the madness. My pleas are ignored once more.

Jake lowers the hydraulic lift, as we wait with bated breath. The water level is only slightly improved, and there are further complications. Lifting the pool has caused the pool to separate from the plumbing, creating a small crack in the pool wall. The pool heater is now inoperable.

After years of wishing for a pool, I have one: a lopsided, fractured hole in the ground that cannot be heated and is surrounded by mud.

Instead of the standard pool deck, a narrow pathway of fake, plastic grass runs from the patio to the pool. It is the perfect caveat to the project from hell. I refuse to purchase new outdoor furniture, because I won't be spending time in this backyard ever again. My beautiful yard has been destroyed. It is a nightmare.

Chapter 15
December 2013

IT IS BECOMING DIFFICULT to hold on to this marriage, as we continue down a slippery slope. Jake's harsh words continue to multiply. His swearing increases by twofold, and he says inappropriate things in public, trying to be the humorous guy in the crowd. What he doesn't realize is that oftentimes people are not laughing with him. They are laughing at him. His inappropriate posturing in conversation is becoming an embarrassment, and it's not the first time I've seen this happen with Jake. I am watching him slowly unravel before my eyes, not just at home but everywhere. I am more embarrassed for my husband than I am for myself.

Regardless of my clearly staked boundaries, Jake crosses them without reservation. He doesn't yell or raise his voice in the slightest. Instead he has begun to execute his sharp tongue with precision through texting. These demeaning words are silent to everyone but me, and they make no sense in a grammatical context. I can't justify how "bitch whore" or "female retard" could be part of a conversation with a woman, especially his wife.

Sometimes I just want to shout back at him, and I often do, for it's impossible to turn a blind eye when your phone is buzzing with insults during a disagreement. But more often than not, I resort to silence. It is my only defense for a man of harsh words. Slowly, I become lost in my own shame for being so compliant.

He blames me for his harsh words, implying that I deserve a verbal thrashing for upsetting him in some way. Apparently, I have become responsible for his emotional discord.

Before I know it, I am living in a fog of sorts, unclear about what is happening to this marriage of ours. Gradually, I start to lose my footing in my own home, slipping into uncharted waters. Walking on eggshells becomes my new normal.

If you are an outsider looking into our marriage, you will see only his sense of humor and his admiration for me, because the ugliness is reserved for behind the scenes; it is usually delivered through the buzz of my cell phone. I haven't yet recognized that my confidence is gradually disappearing. Instead, I push past it, trying to leave the lingering thoughts behind me, as I enter a pattern of cycles with my husband that will leave me dazed and confused.

When Jake is in a good space, I feel hopeful that things will be okay. His humor and affection are what I live for in our marriage. But when he's off the grid, when the dark cloud looms overhead, then I strategically run for cover, avoiding even casual conversations with him. It takes only one small move or one wrong word on my part for him to begin another cycle of loathing toward me, forcing me back into hiding. Sometimes he might not react immediately to a perceived offense. His twitch might go unnoticed, but it builds over time, often leading to verbal outbursts at inconvenient times.

In these circumstances, I pacify him to avoid a confrontation or embarrassment in front of others. "No worries, Jake. No reason to get upset," I say quietly. My calming words become an avoidance strategy, leaving me to feel as though I'm living in the belly of the beast.

Our nights on the couch watching movies are becoming rare, as I spend more time alone, working late in my home office while waiting for him to drift off to sleep. My sleep pattern is slowly changing to unrest and more anxiety, not yet realizing the danger that awaits me on this path.

I carefully place pillows down the middle of the bed, claiming I need them to cushion my knees, creating a pillow barrier between us. I no longer place my hands on his back, as I used to love to do. Instead of curling my body into his arms, I avoid him when he turns toward me. Yet, I still hold out hope, determined that our problems are occurring early enough in our marriage that we can rescue ourselves . . . somehow.

Gradually my house is being dismantled. Unfinished projects and unexplainable holes in the walls appear throughout the house. The basement bathroom remains torn apart, with no sign of a plumber or completion date. The basement ceiling is ripped apart to reroute air-conditioning vents that should never have been directed to Dylan's basement bedroom; this has caused the main central air unit to implode. Holes in the basement ceiling are left open without being patched; instead they are stuffed with dirty rags. But there is no rhyme or reason as to why the holes were made in the first place. The bottoms of my solid wood interior doors in the basement have been cut with a dull handsaw to allow his cat to travel from room to room through closed doors.

Gaping 8-inch holes remain in the garage wall from a recent sledge-hammer mouse hunt Jake went on. Clearly the mouse won, since the gaping holes remain open, creating a gateway for more mice to enter the interior walls to nest. The new kitchen wall oven I purchased is still not framed or attached, so it rattles every time the oven door is opened and closed.

My head spins when I think about the constant disrepair. Walking through the basement, I notice hundreds of dart holes in the drywall and knife marks on the solid wood doors. Apparently, someone used the drywall and wood doors for target practice.

After discovering the knife marks in the wall, I find Jake upstairs and ask without hesitation, "What are those holes in the basement wall? This is my house! It's a wreck since you've moved in here. Please, I'm begging you to stop trashing the house!"

He smirks. "Whatever."

Walking through the basement the next day, I find more holes; this time the darts and knives have been left in the wall, delivering a message to me loud and clear: "Don't poke the bear, for you will suffer consequences." With all these unfinished projects and house damage, I'm in over my head more now than ever.

I approach Jake carefully, waiting for the right time to make a request. "Is there any chance you could finish the basement bathroom? It's been months, and it seems to be getting worse, not better." I don't know why I bother asking. I'm well aware what the response will be.

"It's on my list. If you want it finished, then do it yourself," he replies tensely.

The bickering begins as I respond, "You're the construction guy. All I'm asking is for you to finish the projects you started. For Pete's sake, finish at least one of them."

He claims to be a master carpenter and contractor, but these aren't simple do-it-yourself projects. Most require a professional crew, a team he refuses to hire. My life continues to be driven by anxiety, while I try to make sense of Jake's personality change. I watch as my once-beautiful upscale home is ripped to shreds with no sign of it being repaired anytime soon.

My husband and my marriage seems to be following the same path.

Chapter 16
January 2014

JAKE'S EVENINGS NOW INCLUDE drinking a bottle of wine by himself. Sharing a glass of Merlot, as we did at the beginning, is no longer an option. I have learned that Jake isn't a happy drunk. He is a nasty drunk, and I am forced to be on high alert, keeping my distance and monitoring him from afar. Something is drastically wrong.

I try to keep our conflict from Zoey and Dylan. I'm sure Zoey is aware. Whenever Jake's dark clouds roll in, I have been known to pre-warn both kids to stay at a friend's house, keeping them away from his dark side. A disparaging text cycle starts slowly after our conversation about his drinking.

"Yes, I drink too much. Yes, dear. Whatever you say, dear."

Eventually his texts grow more unpleasant. "No fun partying with you. You're boring. Everyone around the house hates you. Your kids don't like you. My kids hate you. Your brothers don't like you. You are a worthless bitch. Good luck with your sad life when I move out."

This repetitive verbal cycle goes for another few rounds, sometimes for an entire day or more.

In an effort to put me on notice that he is looking elsewhere, he posts rental properties on social media. Aside from the initial sting, it doesn't really upset me that much. In my mind, I think, *Don't stay, Jake. Just go and make it easy on us both.*

When I show some backbone or create boundaries, he threatens harsher consequences, such as calling the police or my children's schools to falsely report them for drug use. After a while, I endure these cycles in silence, trying to avoid the possibility that he will eventually follow through with his threats.

My contempt is slowly building. I question my decisions. How could I endure the verbal turmoil and fail so miserably in my choice of this man? I regret not barricading the bathroom door on the day he moved in. I feel like a coward for not forcing him to take his truckload of crap back to the chaotic house he came from. I am angry at myself for turning the other cheek in return for a moment's peace, rather than standing firm on my principles and established boundaries.

On the flip side, I'm taking mental notes, making plans, and working hard to keep my head above water. I want to be prepared, because when this thing implodes, it's going to be a real shitstorm, and I want to be well protected when it happens.

As months progress, Jake's newest behavior—crude gestures—adds to the difficulty in our communication. The standard jerking-off gesture becomes a common occurrence; he uses it when I am speaking, trying to make a point, or even asking something as simple as, "Can you get my car fixed this week?" More crude gestures usually follow when he disagrees with me. If I ignore him, then he resorts to farting and burping loudly, until I'm forced to leave the room in disgust. This strange behavior coming from a grown man appalls me. In my eyes, it demeans him, but to Jake, his antics seem to empower him in some weird way.

A new cycle of passive-aggressive behavior begins, usually rearing its ugly head at night. He likes to turn up the heat after I've gone to bed, so I wake up sweating in the middle of the night in an overheated house, or he adjusts the air-conditioning to its lowest point, freezing us in the summer. Other times I wake to find all the lights on in the house, forcing me out of bed after midnight to turn them off.

These are small items to fret about, but it happens time after time, and it becomes clear that he will leave no stone unturned in these abnormal, manic cycles.

Once a cycle ends for him, he returns to being the loving, happy man I married. He will tidy up a few house projects, take me out for dinner, or buy one of my kids a car. It's hard to predict the scope of any given apology, but this doesn't mean he's remorseful. It just means the matter is to be put to rest, once I receive his standard text: "I love my wife"—a term I am growing to despise.

Each morning, I recite the same silent prayer, "For the love of God, please, let me find some peace today!"

Yet, at any given moment, for whatever reason he deems important, I face the risk of more painful texts. My hands shake as I endure another round, but the trembling slowly diminishes when I remember he's scheduled to go out of town on business this evening.

Kissing me on the forehead, he says kindly, "Sweetie, me and Dylan will be in Philly," as if the disparaging texts never transpired between us just moments before. With an overnight bag in hand, he closes the front door behind him, returning the house to a comfortable lull just in time for the weekend.

Zoey arrives home from school, bouncing through the door as usual, busy with her Friday chatter and weekend plans. Learning that Jake is gone for the weekend, she invites her friends for a girls' night in. We turn on the house lights, I make a quick stop to buy groceries for the girls, and the house slowly comes to life. By nightfall, the house is alive with the presence of teenage girls upstairs and downstairs, with more friends arriving sporadically throughout the evening. This is one of my favorite ways to spend a Friday evening—entertaining a house full of Zoey's friends.

I wish I could feel calmer in his absence, but he lingers in the negative part of my being lately. The girls' camaraderie helps to lighten my mood and put the day's events behind me. I long to be my old single self, able to focus on my own life without the lingering dread of navigating this marital minefield seemingly laid beneath the floors of my home. Tonight, I leave Jake's words behind and try to enjoy the diversion of a girls' night in.

It's my time to connect with Zoey and her friends, get the scoop on the teenage gossip, and enjoy their company. The smell of chocolate chip cookies and brownies baking in the oven permeates the air. A bowl of raw cookie dough is passed around, with everyone dipping in with their fingers. The kitchen is a happy mess, and the chatter is in full swing. They tell me about their teachers, their boyfriends, upcoming concerts, and vacation plans, as their phones beep constantly.

I know my time with the girls is limited. Eventually Zoey will give me the signal to exit the kitchen with the rolling of her eyes. Soon enough, my time at the table has expired. The girls flow into the adjoining family room and into the upstairs bedrooms on the third floor. The house is always filled with laughter when the girls are here. They make it such a happy night, providing a sense of temporary normalcy for me.

As expected, a few lingering texts come from my husband throughout the evening, interrupting my peace of mind. Even as I sit here with this lovely group in my happy kitchen, he manages to reach me with his defeating words from 300 miles away.

"Having a great night without you," the latest text reads.

Bedtime approaches for me. The girls shuffle around the house, with Riley following closely behind them, craving attention from the small crowd that has formed upstairs. I climb into a bed of clean sheets, thinking how much I love the small pleasure of freshly washed linens delivering their faint scent of lavender.

Lately, the simple niceties catch my attention. I search for anything to calm my nerves. My biggest fan, Riley, arrives in my room, exhausted from the evening, and settles into his assigned space at the foot of my bed. I can feel his warmth pressing against my legs, which will soon be numb from his weight leaning on me as he slumbers. I wouldn't have it any other way, especially tonight.

It's 2:00 a.m., and my eyes open before I'm fully awake. I squint at my bedside clock, frustrated to see the time. *Shit! I don't want to be awake at this hour.* The spiteful text messages from my husband are lingering in my mind. His words bounce around in my head, robbing me of rest. I want to sleep and wake up to the morning light, when I can climb out of bed and busy myself. Instead I lie here in the dark, at the bewitching hour, when thoughts and worries tap me on the shoulder to announce their arrival: "I'm here! Time to confront that shame you've got hidden away!"

It's a known fact that the only way out of the nighttime blues is daylight, and I've got a long wait. Riley notices I'm stirring, so he repositions himself to cuddle closer to me. Closing my eyes, I try to keep my thoughts from going negative, refusing to think about the texts.

When I open my eyes, almost an hour has passed. It's now 3:00 a.m. Thank goodness, I have gained another hour of restless sleep, but I've awakened to a more intense sense of angst. My effort to overcome insomnia has failed. There will be no more sleep, just worry. I check my phone for messages. I see two more texts.

"It's so much better here without you."

"Living it up on the town tonight."

He is putting me on notice that today the texts will most likely continue. I sit up in bed and swing my legs to the floor in response to Riley's panting to be let out for a tinkle. The tops of my feet have recently begun aching during times of stress, so much that I must walk gingerly across the floor until my feet can adjust to the weight of my body.

Twilight gives off a hint of dawn, as I stand at the back door, staring into the dark acres of the woods. I am unintentionally mesmerized and lost in thought, as the sun gradually rises. I have spent another night and now another dawn contemplating the shadows of my marriage. Perhaps today will be better.

The homestead is quiet with the girls all asleep. I prepare a breakfast of chocolate chip and banana pancakes with all the fixings. A breakfast fit for the queens they are.

This morning, Jake's words from yesterday are causing an emotional bruise that only I can see and feel. It is similar to a physical injury when you tenderly touch your wound the next day and say to yourself, "Oh, that's gonna leave a mark." The hostility he lays at my feet causes deep emotional scars. The damage of his words affects my heart, my head, my body, my trust of him, and even my sleep. Yet no one can see my injuries. They are invisible to everyone but me.

These incidents greatly diminish my physical attraction to him. I sometimes cringe when I look at him now. No doubt about it, verbal abuse is a real marriage killer. His apologies are always sealed with a kiss, offering just enough remorse to keep me in the game. I've threatened to leave a few times, an action that tends to break his cycle, but not for long.

Enough thinking about him, I tell myself on this morning. It's time to shower and do something productive, especially on this "free day" from my husband. I turn on the shower and brush my teeth, staring into the bathroom mirror at my sunken eyes and naked body. I admit I look pretty good for my age, regardless of what my husband tells me. At least I'm capable of coming up with one positive thought about myself this morning! I'll take any compliment I can get, even if it must come from me.

I step into the shower, releasing his words and harsh criticism as the first stream of water drenches my hair. I stare through the shower door and out my picture window, appreciative for this hot shower and beautiful view, while making every effort to ignore the dilapidated pool that is in my direct line of sight. His damn words keep circling in my head.

I tell myself, *I'm not crazy! I am not insignificant. I do not deserve this, no matter what he says.* I exfoliate my body slowly and carefully, trying to shed the remnants of his words from my skin.

Stepping out of the shower, I towel myself dry and put on my bra and panties. Out of the corner of my eye, I notice my lipstick on the bathroom counter. I pick it up and, without a second thought, write *Bitch* on the mirror in a lovely coral shade. I write another. *I hate you.* Then another, and another.

Feeling inspired, I hoist myself onto the countertop to reach the sides and upper portions of the mirror that meet the ceiling. I begin to write all the horrible words he has said to me in the last few weeks. Using multiple tubes of lipstick, I let my emotions flow and escape through my fingers and onto the 6 by 10-foot wall mirror that spans the length of the room.

"I wish I'd never moved in here."

"Shut up, you fucking retard."

"You're fucking stupid."

"Einstein, you are really slow."

"I hate living with you."

"Your kids hate you. Everyone leaves you. Your family hates you. Your brothers think you're fucking crazy. Your sister thinks you're a loser."

"I'll burn the fucking house down."

"You are so fucking boring."

"Cunt."

"My friends laugh at you."

"Stop lecturing me."

"Shut the fuck up."

"Fuck off."

"Will be nice living here without you."

"You are not going to beat on me; all you do is beat on me."

"You're a douchebag."

"You should get to the gym at some point."

His hateful words flow from my fingers. The words come so quickly to my mind that I can't keep up. Each word releases pressure from deep within, where it has been stored with nowhere to go, until now.

The remaining steam from my shower blends the lipstick colors perfectly. I use my eyeliner pencils to draw flowers and leaves through the gaps between the words. It is becoming a work of art, displaying the intent of his lethal, debilitating words.

I have no idea what has come over me, not realizing the totality of it all until I've finished. It is there for me to critique, with my own reflection resting deeply in the background and his dark words in the forefront. It's my own artistic way of fighting back. It is quite the masterpiece.

As the day passes, I remember more insults, and I add them to the masterpiece mirror.

"Your father would hate you if he could see you now."

"You're a joke."

"I'm going to look for a new place to live."

"Dylan and I hate it here."

"Don't be expecting any money from me this month."

As vile as the message is, it validates me. I lock my bedroom door to protect my secret creation.

Evening falls, changing the natural light that shines on the masterpiece. Without the sun as its partner, the shimmer from the lipstick has faded. Wine in hand, I admire the new hues of red, pink, and coral shades, echoing my husband's disdain toward me. *How could I love someone who is so hateful?* This is a battle I've not faced before, and it's left me mentally bruised and confused.

Alone in my bathroom, I sift through the emotions. It is the same room where I barricaded the door with my body on the day he moved in, when an untapped fear was forming in my belly. Unfortunately for me, my fears are living up to the apprehensions I had on that day.

My nerves are beginning to get the better of me, knowing Jake will return home tomorrow. What will I do with the masterpiece? It's all I can think about. Staring at it brings me a sense of empowerment, but the anxiety continues to build as evening turns into night. I determine that though I created it on an impulse, I like how it has turned out. It's time I sent him a message. My new intent is to poke him with his own words written for him to see.

The mirror will only infuriate him, I say to myself. I don't want more anger. I want resolution. Do I settle, or do I fight?

I'm growing tired of feeling such stress all the time and of not knowing what lies around the corner on any given day. Some days he greets me with love and affection; other days I'm the handy target of his frustration. On the good days, I'm productive, able to focus on my work, and thinking creatively about how to manage my consulting practice. On the bad days, I am unmotivated and exhausted, just going through the motions, unable to piece two coherent words together or cook a decent meal. I'm forgetful and unorganized, which is completely out of character for me. I've asked him repeatedly to stop swearing and insulting me, so I can think straight, so I can actually like myself and take pride in my role as a mother, wife, professional, and friend.

My short-lived sense of empowerment with the masterpiece mirror diminishes as his return draws near. The fear of consequences seeps into my thoughts, making me feel exhausted and in need of sleep. By the end of the evening and after two glasses of Chardonnay, I make my decision. The masterpiece stays as is.

I've got to get this under control, I tell myself nervously. He needs to understand what his awful words mean, what they do to me and to us. His kids might be used to witnessing his vulgar behavior, but I am not. I am in a state of shock from all this, and I need a ceasefire to begin now. *Let's see how he feels about his own words reflecting at him*, I think.

The next day he arrives home midday, while I'm working in my office. He pauses and says hello with the standard "I'm sorry" look on his face, but he says nothing more as he walks through my office and into the bedroom with his overnight bag. I hear him peeing in the toilet.

I freeze, knowing he's going to see the mirror as soon as he turns around. It's impossible to miss. I sit at my desk within earshot, waiting anxiously. My heart is in my throat, as I regret my decision to keep the masterpiece alive.

The toilet flushes, and a million frantic thoughts rush through me as I ask myself hopelessly, *Why did I start this battle? What was I thinking?*

The only sound I hear is the pounding of my heart and the unbuckling of his belt. Why—oh why—did I confront him with this? Will he feel any remorse? Anger? Shame? How will he react? Shit!

I'm so nervous that I wish I could run out the front door, but I stay and prepare for the worst. I hear him mumbling and shuffling through our closet, looking for something as though he's in a rush. I hear one leg go into a pant leg and then the other. Then I hear the zip of his pants. He exits the bedroom, passing through my office. He is silently seething.

I sit at my desk with purpose, quietly following him with my eyes as he walks toward me, pausing for a brief moment to look at me. I gain whatever strength I can dredge up and whisper directly to him, "I'm not afraid of you."

If he hears my words, he doesn't show it. He walks to the front door, opens it, slowly exits, and gently closes it behind him. It isn't until then that I realize I have been holding my breath. I exhale, feeling the pent-up stress of the last few minutes leave my body. Through the window, I watch him pull slowly out of the driveway.

Sitting frozen in my desk chair, I am too rattled to move. Finally, I find the nerve to rise and walk cautiously through the bedroom and into the bathroom. I find the jeans he arrived home in, crumpled on the floor, covered in lipstick. My masterpiece still shines brightly, but it is altered—smeared in swirls of color, with each word blending into the next. Strangely, the anger of the swirls enhances the artistic quality of the original. The masterpiece shouted his own words back at him, showing him the effect he has on others. He owns those words, and I want him to know it. They don't belong to me. They are his burden to bear.

I stand in awe as I look at the mirror, admiring its profound beauty and the toxic meaning behind it all. From where I stand, I can see the darkness of my pain. When I look deeper, I can see the power of me.

I pick up his jeans, feeling a strange sense of victory and doom at the same time. Unable to take my eyes off the masterpiece, I say out loud to no one, "Find your way, Stella. Fuck you, Jake."

Jake arrives home quietly later in the evening. Feeling empowered, I have left the masterpiece hanging prominently in the bathroom, waiting to greet him when he brushes his teeth before coming to bed. Not a word is spoken between us. My hope is that he will express some type of remorse or at least an acknowledgment of this dire situation. But that doesn't happen. I am silly to think this marriage is going to change for the better.

Neither of us sleeps well that night, tossing and turning while lying back to back on opposite sides of the bed; it's as if we are on opposite sides of the world. He is a man of harsh words and I am growing tired of it. A part of me expected him to wipe the mirror clean when he arrived home—to erase this event from our marriage—but I notice he avoids it. He wants nothing to do with it. I'm getting the sense that he won't be taking ownership of those words anytime soon.

We awake the next morning with a deafening silence between us. Brushing my teeth in front of the masterpiece, I turn to look at him as he attempts to shave without use of the mirror. I glance over in search of a reaction from him, but I see nothing—no depth, no sorrow, and not even anger. He is void of emotion.

Soon after he leaves for work, my phone beeps, and my stomach turns when I see it's a text from him. I don't want to look, but I am compelled to face the inevitable, while I brace for the next round. The text is short and simple. "I love my wife." One moment later, I receive another. "I'm sorry."

The fear begins to leave my body, and I'm relieved at not having to face him in battle today. But the rotting feeling in my gut remains.

Fully aware that his apology is temporary, I accept it, so I can have just one day this week when I can breathe easily. As I expected, his demeanor remains reserved for days afterward. He's being careful with his words.

Quietly, Jake slips into recovery mode. Loving texts begin, which I ignore. Given the circumstances, I feel it's best to remain unresponsive. It's just easier that way.

Soon thereafter, Jake completes a home project to my liking, without me asking. He brings home steaks for dinner, and general conversations begin slowly, as we lie in bed watching TV at night. But it's a far cry from the romance this room has seen of us in the past.

After the masterpiece has been on display for a few days, the time has come to wipe the slate clean. Spraying window cleaner on the mirror, I watch it take on a whole other dimension, as the swirls slowly drip downward, forming new shapes and blended colors with each spray. A part of me is sad to let it go.

Jake speaks not a single word about the masterpiece from that point forward. Yet, I get the sense that he doesn't like to see his hateful words turned on him, exposing his ugliness. Perhaps I have found the Achilles heel of his abusive side. The mirror masterpiece is now out of sight, but it's never out of my mind. For me, it remains a personal triumph, a turning point for me. Creating it has made me more aware and determined to crawl out of the hollow ground I have slipped into.

Chapter 17
February 2014

AS I WRITE MY story, I am often amazed at the level of tolerance I had for Jake's behavior. This is a harsh predicament for me to face, because in no way do I consider myself submissive.

Many have asked me why reaching my turning point took so long. There is no answer for how or why, other than to say that in the midst of emotional abuse, your sense of normalcy shifts from the center, bringing imbalance to all aspects of your once-normal life and altering your emotional equilibrium. Words and actions you never would have found acceptable, now seem like the norm; a regular occurrence. Strangely, they become less offensive and penetrate you less, as your skin thickens from the harsh words.

In survival mode, you live in a whirlwind of confusion. You become conflicted over the simplest of decisions, because in your world, nothing is straightforward. Everything runs the risk of grave consequences. I have learned that confusion and conflict will inevitably ravage the mind and body.

My focus switched from living a happy life to managing my days around my husband's abusive tendencies. Some of his misconduct is overt gestures; others are more passive-aggressive. I get hit from all sides. I spend most of my energy catching my breath and trying to find moments of peace to refuel myself. Short-term decisions—like choosing my immediate battles—are hard enough. Long-term decisions are impossible, since I don't know what the next day will bring. The future becomes like a dense fog. Every wasted mile drains me of energy and purpose.

Withholding financial support is a tactic Jake uses in our marriage with great force. He learned early on that living within my means is a priority for me. I become distraught when he depletes our budget on the first week of the month; it sends my anxiety levels over the top. His method is to overspend and then turn off his flow of finances. His financial contribution will be based entirely on how he feels toward me on any given day. It's financial anxiety times a thousand.

His degrading words define the new me. Sometimes I believe his words; other times I brutally defend myself against them, as I did with the masterpiece mirror. I question my sanity often. My sense of worth is deflated, making it almost impossible to find the exit door. Had I not walked this path of frozen inaction myself, I would never have believed it could happen to a strong woman like myself. On the surface, it all looks good, for this is a private hell in which I live. I know it is of my own doing. It is where I have failed myself.

During the good times, I work hard to warm up to this man; hopeful that we can move past the dark side. Oh, this is a crazy marriage of peaks and valleys, with drastic highs and lows. But isn't that how all marriages are—up and down, and then we land somewhere in the middle?

For me, the middle is nonexistent, and the highs ceased shortly after our wedding. It is the lows where I reside now. I find myself living in a place where not a hateful word goes unspoken. This man of contrasts used to have the ability to make me laugh until my sides split. Now he administers to me a paralyzing fear, forcing me to run for cover when his eyes cloud over.

Through time, I am learning that I can't save the marriage and I can't leave it; each option has its own set of substantial consequences. I am unbelievably stuck.

Jake's home office is located directly off the kitchen, the primary pathway for the daily household traffic. In good times, he is a wealth of information, delivering news and current events from his office chair, with his rich sense of humor. I live for those days when he's funny and silly. He has an easy way about him, and our banter during these moments amuses us both.

The closed office door, sometimes for an entire day, is a signal that warns me of another episode brewing, another turn on the roller coaster. I can't help but notice his door being shut more and more often as time passes.

On one of our good days I made the mistake of surprising him by cleaning his office while he was at work. I wiped dirt and grime from the desktop and put his papers in order. I discarded the used paper plates and old coffee cups. But I was startled to see anger in response. As he had with the mirror masterpiece, in a single backward swipe of his hand, he brought the tidied desk back into disarray, scattering the newly organized paper clips and pencil holders to the floor. The straightened pictures on the wall he made crooked again. The office was in worse shape than before I'd cleaned. He made only one comment to me in passing: "Please don't ever clean my fucking office again."

I've sensed a darker shift in him since the office cleaning. The once-busy weekends we spent outdoors are now nonexistent. The sex is obligatory on my part rather than mutual. It's hard to be attracted to a man who has insulted every aspect of my being. I just dismiss his words and unusual outbursts from my mind. His instability is becoming more prominent, while my tolerance fades.

These shifts confuse me. I am never sure whether to believe his ever-changing rhetoric. What is he for? What is he against? Is he happy with me or angry? His positions on our relationship, parenting, education, or even politics become unreliable, making it difficult for me to discern his actual view on any given subject. He lacks a foundation to build upon. Everything—and I mean everything—changes with the wind from one day to the next.

I find my husband shifting from being interested and complimentary about my special-education consulting career to poking fun at special-needs children. It's almost as though he takes pleasure in shaming me for my work and my clients for their mere existence.

When we began dating, he couldn't ask enough questions about my professional mission, seeking my expertise to help with his son's academic delays and praising me for my dedication. Now, instead of being applauded for my accomplishments, I end up defending my work to him.

Jake takes the educational discord one step further, making it personal by encouraging Dylan to skip large numbers of school days to sleep in—knowing that his absences are not only detrimental to his education but a hot spot for me. In turn, this causes a temporary rift in my personal relationship with Dylan. He has struggled in school, and his father's encouragement to stop trying is an easy out for him, leaving my words and position on the matter a moot point.

Being forced to watch this unfold and knowing that Dylan is not meeting his full potential is reprehensible to me. I've lived with this boy and adored him, yet my bridge to him had been fully barricaded by Jake and his need to undermine his son's future to get to me. Surprisingly, with over thirty-five unexcused absences during his senior year, he is being allowed to graduate. It appears that self-sabotage is a new fragment of my husband's disintegration, even though it is detrimental to his own child's progress.

Jake's once-friendly demeanor around my children has slipped away. He tells me how rude and untrustworthy my kids are, mocks their private-school educations, and claims I am sentencing them to a life of useless college learning and boring careers.

Jake gleams with satisfaction at any perceived mistakes or wrong-doing on their part. He is eager to recap these, keeping their errors on the tip of his tongue so he can recite them back to me. As is true of every loving parent, the consequences my kids receive from me never interfere with my love and support for them. Yet Jake would prefer I approach each incident with anger, instilling fear in them and doling out heavier punishment. He hopes to build a wall between my children and me. In retrospect, I think he resents my love for them.

Given what I uncover after our divorce, I believe he resents *me* even more.

Chapter 18
April 2014

HARRIS MADE SEVERAL TRIPS home during his first three years of college, but it has been too long since I last visited him in Arizona. I'm excited to be going back to Tucson to spend some time with him in his world. By now, he is a confident young man, living in a fraternity and inching toward graduation. After all my worrying about sending him so far away from home at eighteen years of age, it turns out that his choice of Arizona was the suitable place for him to study.

As my trip to visit him draws near, I find myself suffering from an onset of vertigo, a loss of balance, which has been happening to me frequently in the past year. After numerous doctor visits, I accept the unexpected diagnosis of stress-related vertigo, even though I cannot for the life of me understand how stress can cause these debilitating episodes of dizziness and nausea.

Jake knows that, even on a good day, I get motion sickness when I fly. In one of his kinder moments along this bumpy path of ours, Jake informs me just days before my departure that he has upgraded my airline seat to first class. His soft side shines through every now and then. I love it when he does nice things when I least expect it. It is here, in hope, that I keep my anguished feelings for him.

The day before my Arizona trip, in the flurry of preparing for my extended weekend absence, I make two crucial mistakes in regard to a peaceful household. First, I deny a Naples trip to Dylan, who has asked to take a group of his friends to the condo to celebrate his pending high school graduation.

My answer is an unequivocal no. I remind Dylan that he has missed an excessive number of school days, against my wishes.

My response to the question brings Jake to a slow boil. "Dylan and I will take our own vacation somewhere else. Vacations are better without you anyway," he says.

I am too busy packing to argue, so I ignore his comments, putting them out of my mind. My second strike occurs a few hours later when I pass through the kitchen, where Jake is cooking. Coming up from the basement, I make the mistake of asking him to fix a large hole he made months ago in the basement wall. I cringe halfway through my request, realizing I run the risk of upsetting Jake and beginning another one of his cycles.

As I expect, he responds with aggravation. "Yeah, it's on my list. Don't fucking bother me."

By now, I have become accustomed to these responses, so I continue my request anyway. "Can you finish it before the end of time, please? I'm not sure why the hole is even there. What is the hole for?"

Jake replies sarcastically, as he looks through me, "Just add it to the list, dear—and, by the way, don't ever give me a fuckin' list."

I prepare for the cycle by retreating to my room, thanking my lucky stars that I am heading out of town early the next morning.

That evening the silence is broken, and his text messages begin. Step one of the cycle—verbal abuse—is officially in effect. A tornado of consequences will soon follow in one form or another. I know it is bound to happen. I am just hoping to get out of town before it implodes.

"So, no Naples trip for Dylan? I guess I'll be looking for somewhere else to live. Thanks for fucking up Dylan's graduation plans. You're so much fun to have around. Can't wait until you're gone."

I refuse to respond, still focused on getting out of town unscathed at 5:00 a.m. tomorrow.

We go to bed silently, with our backs turned on each other. I try to calm my nerves and pray for sleep, knowing I have an early morning flight to catch. I rise at 4:00 a.m. to shower, still holding on to the hope that we will be kind to each other before I leave. That way, he will drive me to the airport, saving me lots of time by dropping me at the door. Every minute counts with an early morning flight.

We both rise early, giving me hope that a ride might still be an option, but when I wheel my suitcase into the kitchen, I find him in his office with his door closed tightly. And so, step two begins: being discarded and ignored.

I don't bother asking him for a ride. I ramble past his closed office door, dragging my suitcase down the flight of stairs, plopping it heavily on each stair. I drive myself to the airport. As I pull away, I feel such relief to be apart from him. I pick up my phone, sending Zoey a text, reminding her that she had promised to stay at a friend's house for the weekend.

Halfway to the airport, I realize I am driving much too slowly for an open highway at this early hour, an odd occurrence for someone like me who has a heavy foot. Lost in the shadow of my marriage once more, I have no sense of adventure this morning for a trip I have been excited about for weeks.

Even though I know I have the right to speak up and make requests to my husband, I scold myself for not being more strategic. The trip to Naples for Dylan was a definite no, but why didn't I stop there? Why did I have to ask Jake to fix the hole, when I knew it would just upset the apple cart? Why was I always second-guessing myself? Why did I no longer have a voice in my own house? On this beautiful morning, filled with anticipation for my trip, with the Boston skyline ahead of me, I am fighting with my own conscience, trying to make sense of it all.

As I settle into my first-class seat, I remember his kind gesture of making sure I was taken care of in-flight. I find myself wondering,

Should I send him a text? We usually do when one of us travels. Should I send our standard "Wheels up, love you" text in an effort to soften him?

The flight attendant is giving the takeoff orders for the first leg of our flight to Dallas and then on to Tucson. Holding my phone, I am contemplating what to write when I feel the vibration of a text coming through. I see his name and think, *Aw, I knew he would text me something nice.*

As I open his text, I read his simple message: "I hope your plane crashes."

I gasp and shut off my phone just as the plane taxis down the runway. Within seconds, I am airborne in my comfortable first-class seat, with warm towels, a mimosa in hand, and a text on my phone wishing me and everyone else on the flight a devastating death.

Trying to forget my personal turbulence at home, I force myself to drift into the music coming through my headphones, leaving thoughts of him behind on the ground in Boston. There's never a calm moment in my world anymore. As usual, he has skillfully completed step three of the cycle—using humiliation or fear. Today he chooses fear.

Getting lost in my music is becoming one of my coping strategies; it provides me with an escape and builds the strength to step farther away from him. But today the music does little to soothe me. As the lyrics serenade me, my hands and feet tingle in pain. My body is signaling me once more that my stress level is going into overload. The mental anguish makes it almost impossible for me to bend my fingers and toes. I close my eyes so those around me won't notice my despair. I cry silently and without tears, as I have learned to do.

No one can see my emotional bruises, my fear, my sorrow, or my shame over another failed marriage. Only I can. It has come to the point where I have no delusions about my predicament. I know it is going to take the grace of God to get out of this mess unscathed.

The only comfort I can find for this leg of the flight is knowing that with every second that passes I am flying farther away from him. In my heart, I know his reign of emotional abuse is far-reaching, so it doesn't matter where I go. He always finds a way to poke me. As the plane circles the Dallas airport, where I'll change planes, my stress returns, not because of my fear of flying but my fear of turning on my phone.

As we descend and glide down the runway, I turn on my phone, anticipating something mean waiting for me. I am ready to follow my usual plan: quickly scan his messages and then delete them, getting it over with so I can clear my phone of his vile words.

As predicted, more texts greet me in Dallas.

"So nice around here with you gone."

"Why don't you stay in Arizona?"

"I can't stand having you around here."

"Hope you had a shitty flight."

"Take your time coming back. Your family hates you."

Such hatred. I delete the remaining texts without reading them. As much as I want to respond, which I often do, I just can't this time. I am on the other side of the country, away from him for an entire weekend, and Zoey is staying in the city with friends. I will not allow my husband to dominate my time with Harris.

Calling Zoey from the runway brings me relief when I hear her voice and her jokes, along with her weekend plans.

With a few clicks on my cell phone, Jake is now blocked, unable to reach me through my cell. Applying the no-contact rule brings me instant relief. No phone calls, no voicemails, and no texts. My connecting flight to Tucson is stress free. When I land, the only text I receive is from Harris. "Welcome to Tucson, Mom!"

Normalcy—oh, how I miss it.

Harris greets me at the airport with a hug, and my tired heart melts. He'll always be my little boy, no matter how handsome and mature he is, as he stands there before me. He is tanned and relaxed and has taken on the Arizona college lifestyle nicely. I'm thrilled having him all to myself for the weekend, as we visit the Arizona-Sonora Desert Museum, enjoy dinners at the local restaurants, and stroll together through the university campus in the desert heat.

His fraternity house is far different than I expected. It's a beautiful old, stately home on the outside and a filthy, disheveled, happy place on the inside. Harris' fraternity brothers call out to others as a sign of respect and fair warning: "Mom in the house!"

Every young man I meet shows his best.

"Hello, Mrs. Jacobs. So nice to see you, ma'am."

I am elated to hang out with this adult kid of mine.

As my Arizona weekend with Harris nears an end, I dread going back to Larington to face my husband. I know he will be calm by the time I land in Boston, but my patience is wearing thin. How can I be so exhausted from him?

Wheels up! My phone is still blocked from Jake's calls, still following the no-contact rule. I am determined to relax on the flight home. There's no use getting all upset with more texts about crashing planes.

With earplugs in, Wi-Fi, and a glass of Chardonnay in hand, I settle in for a smooth flight. I figure social media will be a good way to pass the time. My scrolling lands me on my favorite animal shelter page. There on the front page is an injured eighty-pound black Labrador Retriever named Bella, with a long, sad face and hollow eyes looking straight into mine. Bella was wounded when they found her living on the streets. She has a torn anterior cruciate ligament (ACL) and desperately needs surgery, structure, and love. The shelter is looking for a foster home where she can heal from her ACL surgery. I don't know what comes over me, but midair, at 40,000 feet, I click the "Foster" button. Within minutes, I receive a response. "When can you come and pick her up?"

"How about tomorrow at noon?" I reply.

As soon as I send the reply, I regret it. Oh, geez, what have I done? Riley will have a nervous breakdown with another dog in the house. Jake is going to have a fit.

But something inside of me doesn't care. The dog is coming home with me.

Just as expected, I arrive home from Arizona to the last phase that is standard in his cycles: redemption. I encounter a loving husband, a spotless house, a full refrigerator, and candles lit through the kitchen. Today I feel differently about this repetitive phase. I'm just plain tired of the emotional chaos.

I roll my suitcase to my room to unpack and find $500 in cash on my nightstand.

"Spending money," he says, as he walks up behind me, putting his arms around my shoulders.

I cringe as he steps closer. Lately, his arms wrapped around me make me feel terribly confined.

Counting the cash, I utter a quiet, "Gee, thanks" and wiggle out of his grasp to begin unpacking. Meanwhile, he chats about his weekend and how much he missed me. There's no apology from him nor a word spoken about his texts.

"How was your flight?" he asks.

"Great. Thank goodness, I didn't crash. You never know when that might happen."

He doesn't even flinch. I offer no details of my weekend; I speak no words of Harris. I am starting to keep my life private from Jake, even though I have nothing to hide. I want to be emotionally separated from my husband as much as possible.

In the aftermath of his cruelty, Jake works hard to make up for the damage he's done, but he avoids admitting guilt. For the next few weeks, he focuses on purchasing a car for Julia and shipping his pickup truck to Arizona for Harris to use. That soft side of him shines through once more. I can see how much he wants to win back my trust, or at least my forgiveness. Perhaps this is the only way he knows how. His efforts, while not impressive to me, are appreciated by Harris and Julia. My kids are enjoying the benefits, and I don't stand in the way of it happening.

The next day, I arrive at the animal shelter an hour early to meet Bella for the first time. She is tired, untrusting, and in pain from the surgery. After I sign the papers, she hobbles to the car on three legs, and we are off to break the news to everyone at home.

Bella is thrilled to hang her head out the window and breathe in the fresh air. I know at that moment that I will never return her to the shelter. It wasn't my intention originally to keep her, but within minutes I know I will find her the right home. If not, then she will be mine and I will be hers. I fall in love with Bella before we reach my driveway.

They have a fond term for this kind of love at the shelter. It's called a *foster fail*. Yes, that describes me, a foster fail, and I'm proud of it. I don't tell anyone at home about my decision to keep Bella. I just introduce her as a foster, knowing that they too will fall in love with her. Bella enters, sniffing the corners of the house, while Riley looks at me as if I have stabbed him in the heart. After a few short weeks, he finally allows Bella to step onto the carpet under my desk. Baby steps. From that moment forward, we are the three amigos.

Chapter 19
May 2014

THINGS ARE GOING A tad better with Jake since my return from Arizona. We are in a good cycle, a time of rest before the next storm. The vulgarity has decreased, and the verbal thrashing has come to a halt. To have peace in the house is a nice change, and I'm doing my best to hold on to what little faith I have left.

We have gravitated back to the outdoors, returning to kayaking the rivers and hiking the early spring trails, but I hesitate to go too deep into the woods with him because I have grown to fear him. Yes, I am afraid of my husband. This is not an easy thing to admit. If we make plans to go somewhere I will text our destination to one of my kids or my mother. I don't tell them why I'm checking in. I just do it to make myself feel safe. Lately, I prefer to spend shorter amounts of time with Jake on smaller excursions. I'm on guard and afraid that too much togetherness will lead to discord somehow, and I don't want that discord to arise when we are in the deep woods or on a riverbank somewhere.

Jake and I walk Riley and Bella on weekend mornings through the expansive Larington Academy campus, making our way to the town center for coffee and tea. Sitting on an outside bench, we observe small-town America. Young mothers push strollers with coffee in hand;

children proudly wear their soccer or baseball uniforms, heading for the candy store; and foot traffic passes in and out of the small shops, creating a vibrancy of commerce.

As I watch, I realize that I have experienced at one time or another all the things I am observing with these young families, but it seems as though those happy moments were from a different lifetime, completely separate from who I am today. The normalcy of this town center community makes me feel all the more toxic as I sit here watching the world pass by. It's as if this secret life I'm living might detonate at any moment without notice, splattering my blood, guts, and shame on the pavement for all to see. I will be exposed for the fake, happily married woman I claim to be while shielding my husband from the exposure of his mean streak. It dawns on me that in the midst of all these people around me, I am in hiding. I am completely alone, and I don't know how to save myself.

It is while I sit here with my husband, during a rare calm moment, that I realize it is unequivocally impossible for my life to ever return to a state of balance while I am with him. It's only been a few years, but it feels so unrelentingly long that I've forgotten what peace of mind is like—until now, sitting here looking at the people around me who are enjoying an uneventful morning. Oh, how I long for uneventful, for not having to worry about consequences and cycles and hiding.

My abused brain struggles as I silently analyze both sides of the coin. I look over at him sitting next to me. He smiles warmly and kisses me on the cheek. Yet, living with him is like running alongside a moving train, not sure whether to hop on board, but ready to do so at a moment's notice once I am assured that the train isn't about to derail. I'm living for the short term, not the long, and the intensity of this marriage is slowly killing me. I know too much about Jake's inconsistencies to make any sudden moves one way or the other with these thoughts that are rambling through my head. So, I sit in silence next to him on this bench, with Riley and Bella at my side, on this beautiful morning in the town square.

This dilemma I face concerns the quality of my life. I've prayed for our marriage, and I've yelled ultimatums. I've forgiven him. I've ignored his actions and stood shoulder to shoulder to fight him. Right now, I'm skeptical and will remain that way until further notice. I wish we could share calm moments like this more often. Deep down, I know that is not possible.

After weeks of smooth sailing, I open our cable bill one day to find a balance of over $1,000 for the month. Not only did my husband reinstate the in-house security cameras without my knowledge or permission, he has taken the liberty of upgrading our television cable to include every channel available—in addition to spending over $300 on rented movies and gaming in one month's time.

Something as simple as a cable bill can wreak such havoc in my life, just as other simple things with this man can become so complicated. Within an hour of opening the cable bill, I cancel the security cameras (again) and delete the premium channels he added. Movie and gaming rental privileges are blocked, and the password is changed, making me the sole manager of the account.

Now I face a delicate conundrum. How do I approach my husband without provoking him? Do I wait and watch it unfold as he channel-surfs this evening after a few glasses of wine, or do I address it with him now over the phone?

In a normal marriage, the couple would discuss and perhaps argue, but in the end, they would resolve the dilemma. Sadly, I don't have that luxury. I must first determine the approach, then examine all possible repercussions and, more important, devise an exit plan should things go bad. I plan these conversations around the children's schedules, making sure they are not home when they take place. I have become an expert on creating avoidance strategies while formulating how I can stay a step ahead of him. It has become a full-time job.

Zoey is away overnight, so I decide to talk to him now. I know this phone call is going to be either short or filled with expletives. Honestly, I don't care which occurs.

Silence greets me from his end of the phone after I explain the $1,000 cable bill. I tell him the cable services have been reduced, and I will hire a private contractor to remove the cameras once and for all. Instead of filling the silence on the other end of the phone with more explanations, I just let the silence hang in the air.

Before hanging up, he utters only one sentence: "You're ruining my day with your bitching." The line goes dead. Our brief honeymoon period has officially ended. And so, it begins, back to the cycles. Step one will arrive shortly.

Dreading his return home, I am relieved to receive a text from him mid-evening, informing me he will not be coming home for the night. "Not sure if you noticed, I'm not home. I'm at a bar, having fun for a change, watching cable. Won't return until the cable and security is reinstated."

I text back. "I hope the bar has a bed and a pillow for you."

My joint pain begins almost instantly after I respond. *Welcome back, anxiety*, I think. I have chosen this battle carefully, even though I know I'll pay a heavy price. What will the consequence be? I do not know. Sometimes I just have to fight back. Today is one of those days.

I walk around the house to calm my nerves, wondering whether the security camera shut-off was instantaneous on my request or if a lead time was needed. Feeling grossly exposed, I hang dish towels over every security camera in the house. I wish I could rip the cameras out of the walls. Until now, he has been able to watch us from anywhere, without my permission or knowledge, from his phone. I am no longer comfortable in my own home nor am I comfortable with his growing paranoia.

Disgusted with the entire situation, I head to my bedroom, hoping there are no hidden cameras there. I am feeling like a prisoner, wondering whether he is watching via some other capacity. I am afraid to undress and crawl into a hot bath, pondering what pair of eyes might be on me.

My anxiety increases as the night wears on. Hours of silence from him means he's brooding, which will somehow result in big problems for me. My stomach is upset. I can't think straight. I drift off to a troubled sleep, reduced to scolding myself once more for speaking out of turn about a simple cable bill.

Well past midnight, my phone buzzes, waking me out of a sound sleep. Struggling to awaken while reaching for my phone, I manage to knock over everything on my nightstand. My heart sinks, as I read his text. "Seeing that you threatened to lock me out of the house, I have contacted the police, and I will be there with a police escort."

Oh, hell, I think. He said he wasn't coming home.

In an effort to deflate the situation, I text him back. "You said you weren't coming home, so I locked up."

Within fifteen minutes, he is home, filled with liquor and anger, but without the threatened police escort. I lie in bed deep under the covers in preparation for his arrival, faking sleep, doing whatever I can to avoid an outburst. I smell the alcohol as he climbs into bed. As expected, he has executed his passive-aggressive sabotaging of the house before coming to bed, purposely leaving all the lights on and turning the heat up to an uncomfortable temperature.

He climbs loudly into bed, shaking the mattress and tugging the covers away from me, getting his message across. Within minutes, his cat jumps onto the bed. I had already put the cat downstairs for the night, so Jake must have let him up, knowing the cat is nocturnal and will spend the night wandering and meowing if not contained in the basement. It's clear that Jake isn't going to take care of the cat, and I'm certainly not going to ask him to.

I move carefully, so as not to disturb Jake. I pick up the cat, which I adore, and take her to the basement stairs, closing the door behind her as I do every night.

When I return to bed, Jake rolls over, looks at me with glazed eyes, and says, "You threw the cat down the stairs. I'm calling the police."

I can't believe my ears. I've been an animal lover for as long as I can remember. I lie in bed, in disbelief as he dials 911. I can hear the police answer on the other end, "Nine-one-one. Your call is being recorded."

Jake calmly says, "I need a police officer here at my home. My wife is abusing me and my cat."

Despite my tears and begging him not to call, three Larington police cars are in the driveway within minutes, lights flashing at 1:00 a.m. As they arrive, I watch the neighbors' lights turn on, one by one, illuminating the commotion. He smiles at me as he opens the front door to greet the officers. For better effect, he walks outside, speaking loudly to them so the neighbors can hear. My stamina is shaken, and my dignity is shattered. He has accomplished his mission once more— to embarrass and control me in any way possible.

Engulfed in shame, I sit on the side of my bed in my pajamas. My face is swollen with tears and despair. Two male police officers enter my bedroom to question me, standing in front of me with arms crossed.

I don't know why, but all I can focus on is their dirty boots standing on my white bedroom carpet, a strange focal point, to say the least. Perhaps it's a diversion from the dysfunction I'm facing. I can't wait for them to take their dirty boots off my carpet.

After talking with me, the police instruct Jake to either leave the premises or spend the night on the other side of the house. I lock my bedroom door and hug Riley and Bella, who are now frantic from the pandemonium. They nervously nestle themselves against my body. I thank the stars above that Zoey is sleeping at a friend's house. Within fifteen minutes of arriving home, Jake has managed to do so much damage.

The message my husband wanted me to learn is loud and clear. If I want peace, then never again should I cancel the cable, for it is an arrestable offense. Everything, and I mean everything, places me in jeopardy.

At this point, the earth beneath me seems unable to hold my weight. I can feel how unsteady the ground is, and I'm looking for something to hold on to, just in case it caves in altogether. If I go under, I might not come back up alive.

Chapter 20
June 2014

SINCE HE ACHIEVED HIS goal during the last 911 call, Jake has stepped up his game by using the 911 tactic repeatedly, adding a new form of fear and humiliation to his repertoire. He's focused on locking in the control with more extreme measures. This new technique is by far the most horrifying of his abusive practices to date—far worse than the verbal abuse, financial sabotage, hidden cameras, GPS car monitoring, and computer stalking that he likes to utilize. I am terrified of the police invading my home again for all to see, and I am even more afraid to know that my husband's motivation is to have me arrested and removed from my own home. He has discovered my fear, and he has every intention of hitting that sweet spot every time.

If I refuse to back down from an issue or when I withdraw into silence, he'll make the 911 threat and eventually the call. Oftentimes he uses his iPhone to film me before calling the police. He taunts me—off camera—hoping to upset me and looking to control me completely. If I go to my bedroom to separate myself, he stands frozen in the middle of the bedroom, filming me sitting in a chair or lying on my bed, as I try to be as still as possible. Any move will be enough for him to cry foul. He works endlessly to antagonize me.

What upsets him the most is when I turn away from him, staying silent and keeping to myself; sometimes this goes on for days. Eventually he works his way into some kind of verbal altercation with me and then smiles as he dials 911 to claim he is being abused. He makes these calls like an expert, knowing exactly what to say. It is tortuous, and he seems to enjoy every moment of it.

I am unable to fight back, knowing the slightest infraction will result in a possible arrest. His alcohol use is noticeable even to the officers as they try to compile what little facts he offers to explain his 911 call. The best they can do is contain him in the basement for the night, advising me to lock the door so he can't gain access to the rest of the house until he either calms down or sobers up. I haven't slept through the night in weeks, instead sleeping with one eye open. Numbness fills my mind, and my body is aching with stress. I am barely surviving—day by day.

His 911 threats are made with broad brushstrokes; they are getting worse as our marriage crawls toward the cliff. I am becoming progressively isolated, virtually hiding from my neighbors due to the police activity Jake has brought into my home. I rarely venture outdoors. I don't even go to the mailbox, fearing a neighbor will want to chat or say hello. Eventually the neighbors stop looking my way. They know something is amiss at my house, and they know it isn't good. So, they do what all neighbors do—turn a blind eye and discuss their thoughts and assumptions privately among themselves.

Who can blame them? I would do the same. I can feel the discord and the negative exposure each time I step outside. I have never felt more despondent.

I live in this beautiful house, but I am sinking deep into depression and feeling emotionally bankrupt. I am afraid to be heard inside the walls of my own home and too ashamed to be seen outside of them. Shame has stifled my ability to speak and be heard. This once strong, proud, single mother and professional woman is slowly deteriorating, close to the point of no return. I see no way out.

Jake is always quiet the morning after the 911 calls, when another of his tumultuous cycles comes to an end. On each of these mornings, I ask for a separation or divorce. His response is always the same: "I love my wife."

He is terrified of being labeled as a sociopath or a psychopath, but this is where my research and therapy have guided me, and I've told him so. But my words only anger him more. I threaten the end of our marriage. I beg him to seek professional help, but he refuses. He sees nothing wrong with his actions, blaming me instead. He claims I abuse him in some way, even though he can't provide any factual proof. Each of his cycles plays out exactly like the others. I feel I can't move left or right, for each way leads me to the most toxic levels of dysfunction.

I am paralyzed with inaction.

After a night in Boston celebrating with her friends, Zoey calls at 10 p.m. with a last-minute request to have her friends sleep over. I am thrilled to have them here, except for one hurdle. I know I have to face Jake, who has settled in front of the television for the night, the same room the girls plan to use when they arrive.

Jake hasn't spoken to me in a few days, for whatever reason he's got in his head, so I know this could be challenging. Every request has to be planned.

When I enter the room, Jake and Dylan are watching television. Walking through the room to let out the dogs, I say to them, "Zoey and her friends are on their way here to watch TV and hang out. Would you mind going downstairs and watching TV in Dylan's room, so the girls can use the family room and the kitchen?"

Dylan jumps up from the floor and smiles. "Sure," he says, as he starts to head for the basement.

Before either of us can exit the room, Jake gets up and comes toward me. I can tell this isn't going to go well. I step onto the patio to let out the dogs, in an effort to break the energy between us.

"We're going to watch the end of this movie here," he states.

I hold my ground. "No, Jake; the girls will be here in twenty minutes. You watch TV here every night. The girls would like to use the family room. Zoey doesn't have a television in her room. Please go downstairs with Dylan or watch TV in our room."

In response, Jake slides the patio door closed, locking it, leaving me outside, standing on the patio.

"Open the door, Jake!" I pound my fists on the door.

Laughing, he walks out of the room. Feeling awkward, Dylan comes over to unlock the door, apologizing for his father's behavior. But before I can step inside, Jake comes around the corner, walking toward me and standing just inches away. Towering over me, he blocks my path and turns on his phone to film me.

As I try to move around him, he cries out as if in pain every time I brush against him. His 225-pound body weight is squeezing me against the glass door. I press my hands against his chest to push him away.

He yells into the camera, "Stop! You're hurting me. Stop! Stop!"

Finally freeing myself, I go to my office and shut the door, trembling. I am trying to figure out what to do with Zoey and her friends, who are on their way. A few seconds later, I receive a text from my husband.

"You pushed me. Dylan is afraid of you. I'm calling the police."

Knowing I have only minutes to spare, I make a phone call to Zoey. "Don't come home under any circumstances. Do you understand?"

"Why? What is wrong, Mom? What is going on?"

"Please take a detour. I will call you as soon as I can. I'm okay. Just give me thirty minutes. I promise I will call you back."

"Mom!"

The police arrive just as I slide my cell phone into my bathrobe pocket. Lights flashing, their vehicles come to an abrupt halt in front of the house and another night of hell begins.

By now, the police officers know me by name. I sit on the side of my bed in my pajamas and bathrobe, humiliated once more, as the police enter my bedroom. I am fed up and frustrated beyond words, yet speechless and powerless. I am stone-faced, unaffected by their presence, while answering their questions.

For the first time, I am blunt and show my frustration. "No, I was not physical. He locked me out of my house and then cornered me. No, I did not push his son. Yes, my husband is emotionally abusive, and I need protection. Yes, I am the sole owner of this house. Yes, I am afraid of him. Yes, I fear for my safety. When will you be finished here? I answer your questions every time you come, yet you do nothing with the information. My daughter is due home any minute. How soon until you leave?"

Despite all the questions and my honest answers, they do nothing except accuse me of being sarcastic.

"Fed up is more like it," I respond.

I return fire with my own set of questions and demands of the police. I have had enough of their inability to protect me. "When are you going to realize what's going on here? How many times are you going to come here before you find me injured or arrest me for something I haven't done? You never take any action, even when I ask you to remove him from my home. Why don't you talk with his son, Dylan, about what happened tonight? He is a nice kid. He'll tell you the truth. Coming here and forcing my husband into the basement for the night is not the solution. You need to remove him from the house. You know his calls aren't warranted!"

The police question Dylan, who has the courage to tell the truth. But then he quickly leaves the scene for the night to avoid the fallout from his father.

On this particular evening, a female police officer happens to be on call in addition to the two male officers roaming my house. She focuses on me, listening to my conversation with the other officers.

As the room clears, she approaches me. "Here is my business card. If you need help, call me, or come to the station and file a complaint."

Finally! I think. I might actually get myself out of this situation alive. Surely the authorities can help me to exit this situation safely.

For the first time, I feel as if someone on the outside has heard me.

Regardless of my answers, each police visit ends the same way: a scolding as they exit, the situation left in the same condition they found it, and me forced to lock my bedroom door and sleep with one eye open. And they continue to leave muddy footprints all over my white carpet!

These police visits weigh heavily on my mind as the 911 pattern continues. My endurance weakens, but, in turn, I am doing a slow burn inside, firing up. I know I have to make a strategic exit sooner rather than later. Marriage with him has become unbearably venomous. However, I know divorcing him will be even worse. I will pay a heavy price for leaving.

The next morning, after the latest night of hell, my phone buzzes as usual with a text: "I love my wife."

How bizarre, I think. The anxiety of living under a roof with this lunatic is slowly killing me.

Chapter 21
August 2014

IT IS BECOMING CLEAR to Jake that I am searching for the exit door, so he takes it up a notch by insinuating that firearms, especially assault weapons, are his favorite new toy. Over the next two weeks, I visit the Larington police station twice in an attempt to file a report on my husband's emotional abuse. I ask for protection from his newest threat: guns and hunting knives.

I left two voicemails for the female police officer who gave me her card but did not receive a response. Each time I visit the police station, I'm met with a plethora of reasons why they can't help me. "It's hearsay," the officer explains. "We can only respond to calls. We can't project what might or might not happen. We can't pass judgment. If you're afraid, then you will have to go to court to file a protective order."

So, the police can't help me to stay safe, but they will come into my bedroom at midnight to question me, only to leave the situation worse than when they arrived. Each time they respond to his bogus 911 calls, they empower him and put me at risk when they allow him to stay in the house afterward. I learn quickly that the police are reactive, not proactive. For a woman in this type of situation, it is no comfort at all, and I am left feeling more isolated than ever. There is no protection for me.

I slip into an all-time low. I am afraid to go out in public, hesitant to even walk through the grocery store. I feel as though my stigma is tattooed on my forehead for the world to see. To me, it no longer seems like an invisible scar; it is evident through my sunken eyes and sallow cheeks. I have cut my hair in a short pixie style, for no other reason than to do something drastic, to make me feel something. I am undernourished and haven't been to a gym or yoga studio since we married. I look and feel like hell.

At this point, Jake is close to achieving his goal in dialing 911. When I hear the same threats repeatedly, and the police are again parked in my driveway with lights flashing, because I showed some backbone, I begin to understand the depths this man will go to in order to be in control. It wears me down to the bone.

What if? What if he finds some crack in the foundation to build a case on? What if the next fraudulent 911 call lands me in jail, and I can't get back into my house? What if I act on my thoughts and physically fight back—because the thought does periodically cross my mind!

Jake brags often about his neighbor's barn that burned down a few years ago. He likes to tell that story but refuses to admit that he lit the match. These are the real queries that go through the mind of a woman who lives with a drip feed of psychopathic abuse from her husband. At some point, she's going to start to believe the dark rumors and the threats, no matter how resilient she thinks she is.

Chapter 22
September 2014

WAKING UP ONE DAY in early September, I know that today must be the day that I plan my escape. No more waiting for things to get better. Fatigue is making me crazy. My body aches every day. I can't spend another night tossing and turning. I must prepare. I need some sound motherly advice and legal counsel as soon as possible. It's time to build my village.

I vowed weeks ago to make the call to my mom. Today is the day. The phone call will be cryptic and difficult for me to make, because my mother likes Jake. He is generally nice to her, always working to charm her.

"Hey, Mom, I haven't seen you in forever, and I've got some things I want to run by you. How about meeting me for dinner sometime this week?"

I accept the first evening she has available and arrange to meet her at her country club for dinner. I arrive early, so I can have a martini before our conversation. She arrives dressed in her favorite color, blue, greeting her friends as she crosses the room, and makes her way to our table. The physical similarities between the two of us are uncanny, including our similar laugh and our preference for the color blue. There isn't another person on earth who knows me as well as my mom and no person I respect more than her. She knows every side of me—the good, the bad, and the ugly. Nothing surprises her.

Our dinner begins with the usual pleasantries. I finish my martini and begin to approach the reason I asked her to dinner. "Mom, there are some things going on at home." Soon I am in the thick of it. "Jake is threatening to litigate for ownership of the house and sue us as a family if the marriage ends. I am devastated at another failure, but I'm making plans to divorce. I didn't want to surprise you with any sudden moves."

Listening intently in her usual quiet way, thinking things through, she asks pointed questions but never judging.

"Does he hurt you?" she asks.

"Not physically, but he does emotionally. I've never been more broken in my life, Mom. I need to get out." I don't have the heart to tell her about the 911 calls.

"What do you need from me?"

"Nothing but your love and friendship. That is all. I'm sorry, Mom. I have failed again, and I'm so embarrassed."

"Don't ever be ashamed for loving someone," she says. "There is always a way out if you choose. Don't hesitate to exit if need be."

We depart with a hug and shared memories of Dad, a topic both of us love to reminisce about. Driving home, I feel a long-overdue sense of relief.

There! I've said it. My secret is out. I spoke my truth. Someone knows now. It's not a dirty secret anymore. I feel a huge weight lifted off my shoulders. It is an empowering, motivating moment.

Two weeks later, I pay a visit to my divorce attorney to make a plan.

My mind wanders, as I drive to her office. I can't believe I'm here again, on the verge of divorce. The quiet life I hoped for has become a tormented existence. My dreams for the future are so far buried that I can't even remember what they are. Survival and avoidance now fill my days, but my quiet rage is building, paving my way to an exit from this nightmare. Jake thinks he has me under his control. He is dead wrong.

Today's meeting turns out to be easier than the one with my mother. This is business. My initial conversation with the attorney begins with a pointed statement by me: "I've been thinking of divorce off and on, but now more than ever."

She asks, "How quickly do you want to move ahead, once you give him the news?"

"At the speed of light. He'll not only make my life hell, but yours also. When this crashes, I want it done fast."

A few weeks after speaking my truth, I feel the strength that I had in my attorney's office and at dinner with my mother diminished some-what. I am overthinking everything, terrified of the unknown, amid the changing of the rules from marriage to divorce. I remember Jake's promise to prevail in the division of assets and sink my reputation if we were to divorce. If he treated me this poorly during our marriage, I can only imagine what the process of terminating the marriage will be like, once he learns all bets are off. Will I survive this?

I am unsure of everything ahead of me. I'm angry with myself. I loathe him far more than I thought possible. I spend the coming weeks examining my part in this marriage. How did I get here? How did this become acceptable—even for a day, an hour, or a single insulting text? What is missing from me that I would not have recognized early in the relationship the true nature of this cruel man? The man he is today is not the man I fell in love with. Or maybe he was a wolf in sheep's clothing from the start, but I was too blind to see. I need to accept my part in all this, realize it, own it, learn from it, and never bring it into my life again. The same thoughts swirl through my head day after day. I hate myself.

I've tried to downplay my marital ordeal with the kids, although it's hard to hide anything from Zoey. She is naturally inquisitive and protective of me. She knows what's going on here, for she's appeared at my side many times with a joke or silly comment to lift my spirits.

Julia has been more strategic in her handling of Jake, especially since she lives out of state. An ambitious athlete, she holds a competitive edge with an opponent and has used this same tactic with him. Jake favors her over the others, but her expressive nature intimidates him. Knowing this, Julia keeps that power in her back pocket when dealing with him under pressure.

Harris has not been privy to my relationship with Jake and I've made the effort to keep him out of the loop to avoid further embarrassment on my part.

I pray every day that my three children will remember my attributes rather than the glaring error in judgment I made in choosing this man.

I barely notice the emergence of autumn. My favorite season is lost on me this year. There are no pumpkins on the doorstep and no seasonal festivities taking place in the house. I don't have the energy. My anxiety escalates to full-blown panic attacks. My immune system is beginning to fail. Simple colds turn into bronchitis and pneumonia. I seem to be on antibiotics all the time to fight off some type of infection. My health is deteriorating as I sink into depression.

I need reinforcement. I want an impartial supporter, not someone who will tell me everything is going to be okay, but a professional who can help me walk over the hot coals to free me from my self-loathing. I need someone who can counsel me, so I never again have to face this nightmare. I can't do this alone. It is time to add another reinforcement to my village. I need all the help I can get.

With a bit of research, I stumble on a therapist who fits my requirements. Initially, she intimidates me a bit. Sharyn is a no-nonsense kind of person, and I'm unsure whether she's going to take pity on my situation or take me to task for being silent and weak for so long. Her questions are direct. "Why are you here? What is it that you want in your marriage? What changes would you like to see in your life?" It takes her only one session to see what I have been unable to.

Before we begin this therapeutic journey, she makes it clear that my personal investment is a requirement of hers. She's not one to listen endlessly. She has input to provide and direction to give. I can see she will have expectations of me. I get the sense that this woman will be able to guide me through this process of freeing myself. I like her style.

Secretly I have the delusional thought that Sharyn might be willing to see Jake and me together as a couple. I'm not sure why I think this. I know deep down my goal is to escape this marriage, but my mind continues to play tricks on me. There are moments when I convince myself that I can somehow save this man from himself. My request for couples counseling is met with an unequivocal no, as she makes it crystal clear that she would like to see only me.

I follow Sharyn's lead as she pokes around my life, helping me to find a starting point. We begin with the story of me, and it isn't an easy subject to address. How do you speak about yourself when you no longer know who you are? What do you say about yourself when you can't figure out what the hell is happening under your own roof, in your own marriage, and in your own mind and body? How do I explain I spent most of my childhood in silence, tucked away comfortably in my bedroom, and here I am again, but this time I'm hiding in my own home.

Buried under my distress is the answer that has yet to rise to the surface. My mind rushes with the thoughts that have been cycling through me for months. "I used to love myself, but now I don't. My current life sucks, and I want my old life back as a single mom, or a new life far away from him. Perhaps we should start small and build from there. I would just like to take a deep breath without feeling as if my lungs are going to explode and my ribs crack open. I would like my hands to stop trembling and my feet and back to stop aching with stress. I would like to listen to the music in my car again instead of driving in complete silence. I would like to execute a simple grocery list from memory while shopping so I know what food to purchase. I would like to feel just a smidgen of positive energy and motivation on any given day."

Instead, I answer Sharyn with the same confusion that I struggle with every day: "I don't know, but I need to figure it out."

As the therapy sessions unfold, I begin to see myself more clearly. The rapport between Sharyn and me allows a relaxed dialog, with my thoughts flowing more freely than I had anticipated. I feel comfortable with her. Her approach lightens the load, as she slowly begins to lift the curtain of my marriage. It is here in her cozy office, session after session, where my eyes open, and my backbone begins to mend itself, preparing me for the tasks ahead.

She introduces me to the terms *psychopath* and *empath*, recommending literature on the topics. She waits to hear my thoughts, taking my lead as to how it relates to my situation. The term *empath* describes me perfectly. Finally, I have a clinical term for the person I've been sleeping next to—*personality disorder/psychopath.*

Reading these books provides my aha moment when I realize quickly that every sentence I read pertains to my life in one way or another.

I have downloaded the books to my laptop, so Jake is unaware that I'm reading them. However, given his tendency of stalking me through keystroke software, I doubt it will be a secret for long. Soon enough, often going to the public library for privacy, I am filling my free time with reading and researching, as my confusion fades before me.

An empath enables others, convinced she can heal the toxic person by putting that person's well-being before her own. Empaths are also the ideal target of a psychopath. It is a clinical term I know little about, but as I learn more, I can see that it describes many aspects of me, beginning in my early childhood years. The more I read, the more my thinking about virtually everything changes.

Here's what I learn.

1. Empaths are spiritual.

2. Empaths absorb the emotions of others. Doing so can exhaust them.

3. Empaths are usually introverts and seek their own space where the energy is clear of activity and free of judgment from others. Speaking from my own experience, I developed this trait at a young age. For me, the energy at our dinner table was emotionally chaotic. Each personality seemed to speak to me without words. I could sense their irritability and the competition at the table of eight people trying to be heard. It was an intimidating atmosphere for me. Solitude was the only way I could unwind. Even today, it is in quiet places where I find true peace.

4. Empaths are intuitive.

5. Empaths have difficulty separating the absorbed energy of another from their own personal thoughts and needs. This is where empaths go into overload, especially in social situations.

6. Intimate relationships can overwhelm an empath.

7. Empaths are targets for energy vampires. Energy vampires consume the relationship, needing the attention to be focused on them. Oftentimes that attention is achieved by negative control over the empath.

8. Empaths seek out nature.

9. Empaths are sensitive to the human senses. Smells, talking, light, and noises are bothersome to them.

10. Empaths have big hearts and are convinced they can help others unconditionally.

I also learn there are three stages of living with a psychopath: (1) idealization, (2) gaslighting, and (3) triangulation. My husband fits all three categories.

Idealization is all about love bombing a new relationship. This new person in your life seems too good to be true. He makes lots of promises. He is a gift giver who will work relentlessly to keep your heart pounding twenty-four hours a day, seven days a week. He does anything to impress you. He whisks you off your feet and refuses to move slowly. He wants to be your endgame, your only option, and your true love. The highs are euphoric, and the lows are nonexistent. There is no neutral ground. He provides adventure and security that you have not experienced before. He demands your undivided attention. You become accustomed to being on the pedestal he has placed you on. His admiration for you is invincible.

What a lovely ride the idealization phase provides, as you freefall into love with an admirer rather than an actual partner. Unfortunately, like all things that are too good to be true, this phase ends, only after he is certain that you have made a commitment. You are convinced he is just as committed to you. But it is here where the delusion begins.

Jake's love bombing overshadowed the few red flags I saw when we moved in together. My body and mind were shouting warning signs to me, yet Jake's coaxing won me over. I have only myself to blame for my ignorance at this stage of the relationship. It was a few months into our marriage that the idealization phase, the love bombing, came to an abrupt halt.

Gaslighting is a form of manipulation and brainwashing. Psychopaths often rely on surveillance, even though it is they who necessitate monitoring. Spying on others with cameras and tracking devices during this phase helps to reduce their paranoia and gives them a sense of control by watching others without their knowledge.

During this phase, unbeknownst to you, a dense fog encroaches, forcing you into a gradual state of confusion. Things you say become twisted. Most discussions are chaotic with the fault always leading back to you. Accusations rest on your shoulders, leaving you to feel defensive at every turn. To keep the euphoric relationship going, you tend to ignore his inconsistencies and the accusations made against you.

The changes are so subtle that you don't know what to think. Over time you begin to question yourself repeatedly, as you are slowly deprived of the love and attention you have become accustomed to with your partner. You ask yourself, "What can I do to fix this? Is it me? Am I crazy? Am I over thinking things?"

Slowly you realize he is losing interest in you, giving you cause to question and blame yourself. You have the urge to make things right, even though it wasn't you who made them wrong. His deteriorating feelings for you are delivered with a vengeance, along with a laundry list of why you are not worthy, leaving you to freefall to earth—hitting the ground with a bang.

You are unaware of how you lost your foothold on the trusting, romantic, and perfect relationship you had within your grasp. Rest assured that the blame will be placed on your shoulders for you and everyone around you to see. This phase lingers as you drift between the good and the bad, hoping that the bond you once shared will prevail.

Triangulation is the hardest to endure. This is when your partner brings someone else into the relationship in an effort to show that you are replaceable and disposable; sending the message that someone worthier will take your place. Managing his intense need for admiration and control are the psychopath's primary objectives.

The triangulation phase usually includes adding another sexual partner to the relationship. I use the term *sexual partner* because the psychopath doesn't feel real love for another person. They don't have lovers; they have sexual encounters. Oftentimes, triangulation doesn't stop at sex. The abuser may search for additional ways to humiliate you in front of others.

I rest comfortably in this moment of discovery, knowing that Jake and I do not fit the typical triangulation mode in regard to cheating. At least we were monogamous with each other. That much I know to be true.

For Jake, it was the 911 calls, bringing the police into our relationship to increase his control over me. It was his favorite method of abuse, intimidating me into isolation from my children, family, friends, and even my neighbors. He enjoyed the power immensely. It is the itch, the desire for toxicity he couldn't live without, and he obtained it at the expense of my dignity.

As I begin to understand these traits, I lie awake at night feeling a shift in my spirit. My confusion is lifting from the dense fog. The more I read, the more empowered I become. My husband sleeps beside me, yet he has no idea of my secret transformation or the plans that I'm laying out, a little bit each day. I am becoming resolute. Knowledge is power.

I am no longer paralyzed with inaction. Instead, I have become a woman on a silent mission. Taking control of my thoughts, I don't worry anymore about his conduct or how rotten he makes me feel. I couldn't care less if he gets better. Rest assured, the time to break free is near.

Chapter 23
October 2014

HOW MUCH OF WHAT happens in childhood affects us later in life? Some therapists like to go far back to some incident that might have affected the decisions that are made today. I'm not a big believer in blaming childhood events for my current problems. I've lived most of my life thinking that what happened in the past should stay in the past. There's no use carrying around a heavy suitcase filled with bad memories or discord. That emotional baggage gets heavier by the day, making it more difficult to think new thoughts and trust new people.

In my opinion, negative experiences can become a cumbersome load to carry day in and day out, year after year, decade after decade. Where is the relief in that? The baggage I chose to leave behind occurred when I was a nine-year-old girl. Surprisingly, this incident, which happened over four decades ago, resurfaced in the last phase of my marriage with Jake, bringing a monumental awakening and hammering the last nail into the coffin of our relationship. After working with my therapist, Sharyn, I now realize that what happened to me growing up did, in fact, affect my life.

Shortly after my parents married in the early 1950s, the family expansion began. A new sibling joined the family every few years until, by the late 1960s, the final count was six kids—four boys and two girls. My place in the lineup was the third child and the first girl. I was a proud tomboy from the get-go, born smack in the middle of my four brothers, with my sister not arriving until I was nine. We were a boisterous bunch—Patrick, John, Stella, Liam, Henry, and Caroline—a handful for any mother to run through on a daily basis. We were a proud, sports-on-Saturday, church-on-Sunday kind of family. The quiet suburban town of Hingham, located on the south shore of Massachusetts, was our hometown and the center of the universe throughout our childhood.

Being the oldest girl in my family, I adhered to the unspoken rule that I would tend to my three younger siblings. For the most part, it was a responsibility I enjoyed. I would often hustle my little brothers to the neighborhood playground to relieve my mother. Taking the shortcut through the woods, I'd walk the same worn path that we used for our neighborhood games.

As we made our way to the playground one morning, I held a picnic lunch in one hand and my baby brother Henry's hand in the other. At three years of age, he needed my full attention to maneuver the path. He was so proud, hopping over large rocks and tree branches, laughing proudly with each jump. Suddenly, I felt someone touch me from behind, and then I felt hands being placed tightly over my eyes.

"Don't scream," he said quietly in an adult voice, as he leaned into my ear, giving me cause to grasp my brother's hand more tightly. "Pull down your pants," he whispered, while still covering my eyes.

The panic of losing my brother overruled everything else at that moment. I was too young to know about rape. Instead, my mind became fixated on the horror of us being kidnapped. I stood frozen in fear, while Henry started to cry.

The stranger's hands moved roughly from my eyes to my neck. "Don't turn around," he said, as he wrestled my pants to the ground.

One of his hands tightened around my neck, and, with the other, he pushed my forehead into the trunk of a nearby tree. The force of his action cut my forehead open, blood from the wound dripping down my nose, as I stared blankly at my brother's shoes. Concentrating on his shoes. Thinking of nothing else. Not understanding the pain that was shooting through my body.

The farther down my pants went, the harder I squeezed my brother's hand. I don't know whether he was screaming because I was gripping his hand so tightly or if he was howling in fear. It was a loud, frantic wailing, as the man behind me struggled with my petrified, frozen resistance.

After one final, desperate shriek from Henry, the man turned and ran away. I tried to pull up my pants but didn't want to let go of Henry's hand. Pulling them to my hips, just enough so I could move my legs, I picked up my brother and ran. I didn't know which direction to turn for our escape out of the familiar woods. I just ran, with Henry screaming and squirming in my arms.

I found myself more frightened during the escape than during the incident itself. I was petrified that the evil man would give chase or pop out from behind a tree in some wicked twist. He'd wrap his hands around my neck once more and rip my brother out of my arms. Was he hiding and waiting for us? I was certain I wouldn't live through the horror; deathly afraid he would kill us both.

I lost my way as I ran through the woods. Stumbling in despair, carrying my brother, who was getting heavier and difficult to hold, I became breathless. Eventually, I found my way onto a familiar street, farther from home than I had hoped. Henry had become eerily silent with wide eyes, as he clung tightly to my hair to support himself as I ran with him.

My arms were exhausted, my stomach retching. I finally put Henry down, pulling him alongside me instead. My mind raced. I was so panic-stricken that my throat began to close, choking on the air I was trying to inhale. I didn't know how much longer I could drag Henry without getting hurt.

Finally arriving home, Henry and I stumbled into the house, breathless. Both of us were covered in scratches and dirt from the woods, completely disheveled, and traumatized. I was gasping for air, as the sound of terror escaped from my throat; I let out a chilling scream that no mother should ever have to hear.

I sat motionless on the sofa with my knees pulled to my chest, as the police asked me questions I was too young to answer. Numbness settled inside me. Still afraid in a deeper, more solitary sense, I remained curled into myself until my nana arrived to sit by my side. Without saying a word, she held my face and kissed my forehead. I was finally able to cry, sobbing out the terror I'd experienced. I remember my father arriving home in a frantic state of mind. His anger and exasperation showing on his face, as he lost his temper with the police who were questioning me. After hours of looking through police mug shots with my nana sitting protectively next to me, I could not identify the perpetrator. I saw his face for only a second when he pushed away from me to run, yet I will remember that glance and that face for the rest of my life.

Those to whom I have told this intimate story ask me how I overcame the ordeal. My response usually surprises them. How can you conquer an experience in which you had no control? How does a parent explain this horrific act to an oblivious young girl and still assure her that intercourse is an act of love?

So, all I could do was to leave the incident behind me. I couldn't erase it. It happened to me, and that will never change. For some reason, perhaps because I didn't understand the concept, I did not fully connect myself to the sexual act that was thrust upon me. I don't remember receiving counseling afterward. I did not go to the hospital, and I don't recall seeing a doctor. The event disappeared into the folds of my life as an unspoken incident. That's what families did in the late 1960s. We didn't advertise this type of thing. Instead, we put it discreetly behind us.

To show how deeply it rooted itself, a few years after the incident, both my fifth and sixth grade classrooms overlooked the wooded path where the terror occurred. Yet, sitting at my desk every day, not once did I look out the window to recap the most terrifying experience of my life that had taken place a few hundred yards away. What I didn't perceive at the time was how or why I became indifferent about it. As I grew into my teenage years, I was not keen enough to grasp the correlation between my chosen isolation at home and the molestation I endured at the hands of a stranger.

I often wonder if therapy would have provided clarity or absolved me from that summer day. In full disclosure, I told my therapist, Sharyn, about the incident. I narrated in a matter-of-fact manner, keeping that day separate from my emotions while telling her the details that still haunt me.

The escape out of the woods was the most terrifying element, and it remains so to this day. As vivid as my memory of the escape is, the molestation remains obscure to me. Some of the few people I've told suggest that I am in denial by blocking out the assault, but I beg to differ. I realize fully what that horrid man did to me, and I see my fading memory of it through the years as a blessing.

My family never spoke of it again. I do not know if my brother Henry was ever told of the trauma we endured in the woods on that day. I like to think that my actions saved him, just as much as his presence and crying saved me.

I hesitate to even tell the story, for I've learned that by doing so I risk becoming a victim in the eyes of the listener. In my eyes, I am not a victim. I am a strong woman today despite the incident.

I understand that a stranger caused a piece of me to be broken forever, but identifying myself as a victim would mean that the man violated more than my body. He would have violated my soul if I'd let him into my thoughts. Even as a young child, I knew I could never let that happen. Forty-five years ago, my nine-year-old self decided to leave it behind. I have honored and not questioned that young girl's decision since.

Chapter 24
November 2014

IT'S NOVEMBER 14, AND winter is settling in. After pouring yet another jug of Jake's hidden vodka down the drain, I decide I've had enough. I'm not sure why this juncture marks the beginning of the end. It just does. My instincts are telling me to stop hiding, to stand still in the moment and let it finally unfold.

Over the last few weeks, my offers for a speedy divorce have been rejected, and his manic cycles are becoming more frequent with each new request I make.

I have a divorce attorney on retainer, I am secretly working with a therapist, and my mother is behind the scenes for extra support. My closest friends are on call and prepared for the crisis alarm to sound. Zoey and I have had many conversations about me ending my marriage, and she is counting the days until the upheaval begins, while still finding humor in the situation.

"We're a team, Mom!" she says with a thumbs-up.

The holidays approach, and I dread facing Thanksgiving and Christmas with this jerk. I'm isolated at home, trying to keep my distance. I am embarrassed to be associated with him in public due to his recent decline in social behavior. I cannot do it any longer.

After sharp words between us and a restless night of little sleep, the next morning I offer one last opportunity for him to seek rehab. But things get twisted again when he accuses me of attempting to admit him to some kind of mental institution, aka therapy. In fact, my true intent is to set the stage by putting a heavy emphasis on an imminent divorce. No matter what I say or how I say it, everything ends up so tumultuous that nothing can possibly be accomplished. He is the master of muddying the waters.

In the middle of our conversation, he decides to divert attention by stripping down naked in the middle of the bathroom as we're talking. Climbing into the shower, he casually looks over his shoulder at me with a final comment that seals our future. "I don't need no therapy. I'd be fine if you'd stop pissin' me off all the fuckin' time."

I respond, angry and impulsive, "I'm filing for divorce, and this thing needs to end one way or another."

He closes the shower door, folds his arms over his chest, hangs his head downward, and stands under the hot shower lost in thought as the water flows down his back.

Every moment of every day, I face anxiety and uncertainty with this man. This short marriage has turned out to be a prison sentence for me. I need to get paroled.

Moments later, I walk back into the bedroom, watching him dry off with a towel. Having no words to add to our previous conversation, I turn to walk away, wanting to avoid further discussion and wondering why I even came back for another round.

"Hey," he starts.

I turn to face him. "Yeah?"

He speaks softly for the first time in a long time. "I love you. I don't want a divorce. I'll go see someone for help."

It has been a long time since his words have shocked me. I look up at him in silence, willing myself to feel compassion after his response, but all I feel is indifference. At this point, I'm looking for a way out more than a reconciliation. Despite my teetering between emotions up to this point, I have already exited, and I think he's known it for a long time.

Am I supposed to rejoice with open arms? I can't. "I think that's a good idea. Get yourself balanced," I say, secretly thinking, *Not a chance in hell that will ever happen.*

A few moments later, he's dressed and ready for work. He reaches out for me. I pretend not to see, so he kisses me awkwardly on the cheek and says, "I love my wife."

I have no response. The day continues like most, just another workday to get through.

About seven o'clock that evening, I notice the time and realize he's late coming home, which isn't unusual, given his work schedule. I like when he's out late. His absence in the house allows Zoey and me alone time without his interference. By eight o'clock, I'm relaxing with my laptop, scrolling through social media, and chatting online with friends about life—an existence they know nothing about regarding my marriage. To them, everything in my world is tremendous. Violation and shame have turned me into a liar because of my endless efforts to hide the oppressed skeleton living in my closet.

As I scroll through Facebook, I stumble on a picture of Jake that he posted minutes earlier. At first glance, I don't think much of it. Looking closer, I see he's sitting at a bar, holding a small sign that reads "Reserved." He's got that up-to-no-good grin that I know so well on his face. Looking closer, I see his wedding ring isn't on his finger, another common occurrence when he's angry and on the verge of another cycle.

Here we go again, I think. *Hold on, Stella. We're in for another roller-coaster ride of consequences.* But this time I refuse to believe it. Not this time, I think. Never again.

Each day the ground beneath me is becoming more solid. For weeks, I've contemplated my next steps with my therapist, although I've done so without a specific time frame in mind. Regardless, I've got things in place. Everything is ready to go. The time is now to hit the exit button.

I close my laptop and stroll through the house, passing through the rooms. Riley and Bella follow closely behind, and the three of us end up in the kitchen. Opening a cabinet, I decide on a bottle of wine and pull out one of my grandmother's vintage wine glasses. Sidestepping to the next cabinet, I grab a box of crackers and then open the fridge for some sharp cheddar cheese. Taking a seat at the kitchen counter, I run my hands over the new granite, feeling its cool, smooth surface against my hands. I pour a tall glass of Merlot, taking time to savor the first sip. I can't help but admire how beautiful the kitchen remodel turned out to be and, in the same moment of appreciation, realize this kitchen will far outlive our marriage.

Lowering the lights and lighting the candles, I relax. Sipping slowly, I pull crackers out of the box, stack each one with cheese, and pop them into my mouth. I pause and drink in silence, feeling amazingly calm. The dogs are close by me in their kitchen beds, looking for me to determine their next move. I tell no one what will transpire tonight. I cry no tears. I feel no anger. I am existing in the moment. I am just being. This quiet reflection calms me and the cheese and crackers are the perfect late dinner.

It's ten-thirty, and the sound of Jake's car rumbles down the back driveway. I'm still sitting in the kitchen on my second glass of wine, with my feet crossed and resting on top of the counter, scrolling through my phone while enjoying strawberry cheesecake directly from the container. My husband comes up the stairs from the garage, looking surprised as he steps into the kitchen to discover me sitting in the chair waiting for his arrival.

I'm sure he thought he was walking into a sleeping household, as he usually does, but tonight he isn't so lucky.

"What's up?" I say cheerfully.

He quickly readjusts his look of surprise. As usual, he's intoxicated and using every ounce of concentration to walk carefully across the room without stumbling. It takes immense concentration on his part to make his way to the kitchen sink to wash his hands. I sit casually, emotionless, watching and waiting to see what will happen next. His speech slurs with each word. I sit casually with a reserved sense of confidence. The ease of my demeanor seems to confuse him. I know, without a doubt, that these next few moments will be decisive and this time, it will be me with the upper hand.

Shutting off the kitchen faucet, he reaches his left hand into his jeans pocket, trying feverishly to get his ring back on his finger with his hand still in his pocket. It's so obvious that I can't help but enjoy watching him struggle.

He looks over to find me observing him, and in the voice I have grown to despise, he slurs, "What the fuck are you lookin' at?"

I stay silent, deciding it's best for me to just sit still a bit longer, watching him take his last breath within our marriage.

"Where were you tonight?" I ask.

"Out. Not with you," he responds.

I look over at a small gift bag he's carried in with him and placed on the counter. "What's in the bag?" I ask in a hushed voice.

"None of your fuckin' business."

I reach over from my chair, lifting the gift bag by the handle with my pinky finger. "I think it *is* my business. Do you mind if I take a look?"

The hatred in his eyes is glaring, burning through me as I open the bag. Pushing aside the tissue paper, I pull out a jewelry box, open it, and find the watch I had hinted about weeks earlier for my birthday.

In his hateful, slurred tone, he says with squinted eyes, "Happy birthday, you fuckin' retard."

My response is unemotional, just as I have felt all night long. I sit back in my chair with my arm swung casually over the seat back, speaking quietly and slowly so his drunk brain will comprehend my words.

"My birthday was fourteen days ago. The window of opportunity for you to give your wife a birthday gift ended on November 1, the day I was born. Today is November 14." I continue with raised eyebrows, as I ask one final question, "Is today my birthday?"

I snap the box shut, toss the watch back into the bag, stuff the tissue on top, and slowly slide the watch back to him.

"We are getting a divorce," I say with quiet determination. I stand and walk out of the kitchen toward the bedroom.

When my back is to him, just as I am exiting the kitchen, he slurs, "I'm so glad you were raped as a kid and no one in your family believes you."

The words stop me dead in my tracks. I'm thankful he can't see the expression of shock on my face. I pause briefly, standing still for mere seconds, as I contemplate turning around to respond, but then I remember that he is intoxicated. Instead I keep walking toward my bedroom, the dogs following close behind. Closing my bedroom door, locking me in and him out, I vow this will be the last time I have to lock my bedroom door ever again. The power he has stolen from me comes rushing back in waves. The time is now. Of that I am sure.

For the first time in months, I sleep soundly that night. I wake in the morning with ease at first—stretching and petting Riley and Bella—until the reality and memory of last night's events invade my solitude, jolting me awake. Jumping out of bed and dressing in whatever clothing is within reach on my closet floor, I quietly open my bedroom door, tiptoeing to scope out the situation. I'm not sure where he will be or whether he is here at all. *Did he leave? Is he sleeping somewhere in the house?*

Soon enough, I hear his drunk snoring on the opposite side of the house. I feel sick again. There he is, sleeping on the family room couch, arms over his head, snoring with his mouth wide open. The cat sits patiently on his chest, staring at him, wishing him awake.

With last night's words ringing in my ears, all I want to do is startle him awake and snap him out of his drunken slumber. I yank the pillow out from under his head, causing it to bounce off the upholstered arm of the couch. Next, ripping off the blanket, I find him sleeping naked, repulsing me.

My voice filled with determination, I say, "Get up. Get the fuck outta my house, and don't ever come back."

Not everyone can put a finger on the exact moment their marriage ended. I can.

From the day he exits the house, something subtle begins to take place. My home becomes calm, predictable, and far less stressful. The bills are manageable again. There is a long way to go to pay off the overdue bills he left behind, but in time I will catch up. Finishing the uncompleted construction and all its damage will take a crew and thousands of dollars.

It feels strange to sleep alone, yet I'm not lonely. I'm grateful for Riley sleeping at my feet, and Bella, who has taken over Jake's spot in the bed, snoring into my ear. Her legs constantly twitch as she runs in her dreams. While she dreams, my nightmares awaken me. I am confused and conflicted with my decision. I have no idea if I will ever be able to shake the torment from my memory.

There are daily emotional landslides that whisk me directly into hollow ground, leaving me to do the slow, emotional climb once more. But I am determined to repeat that climb as many times as necessary to put him and the mayhem behind me.

I'd like to say that I am leaving this marriage like a warrior, but I'm not. It isn't anything like that. I am crawling out. I am emotionally beaten and battered inside, trying to put on a strong front on the outside. I don't feel victorious at all. I am terrified, knowing the damage he still might do in the name of divorce.

Soon thereafter, I am diagnosed with posttraumatic stress disorder (PTSD), related to the abuse that took place in my marriage. I will battle these symptoms for a long time, perhaps forever. My stress-induced vertigo is at an all-time high; I am overcome with nausea each time I turn my head too quickly. My hair is falling out by the handful. My weight has dropped to dangerous levels over the past months. The constant tears have begun to steal the softness from my face. I had no idea, until now, how broken I was.

The strangest part is the difficulty I'm having as I return to normalcy. I can't get through an ordinary day that is void of commotion. How can I be so untrusting of a calm household? Instead I wait for the other shoe to drop. I thought I would find peace just by forcing him out of the house. I was wrong. The threat of him still lives here and it still lives within me.

Since then, I've learned that leaving abuse behind can be difficult; victims are often drawn back to toxic situations and relationships. Just as with drugs or alcohol, the chemistry in my brain was triggering me to return to the dysfunction of my marriage to satisfy the withdrawal symptoms I was having. My body needed to maintain the fight-or-flight chemistry levels it had become accustomed to, and it wasn't going to relinquish those levels easily.

Over the course of the first few weeks of our separation, I'd think periodically of going back to him. The mere thought of it makes me frantic, yet my brain keeps moving in that direction. Healing from abuse, living a life free of toxicity, is like learning to walk again for me.

Keeping my village tight around me, I meet with my therapist multiple times per week, sometimes for double sessions and oftentimes making appointments at the last minute. No matter when I call, Sharyn makes herself available. She knows I am at a fragile turning point, and she does everything in her power to get me through. She brings me back from the darkness, and I will never forget the impact she had on me at a time when I was more lost than I've ever been.

The hours I spend with her are an important component of my recovery. I have never cried harder, felt more pain, or endured more shame in my life. As hard as it is, I begin to shed those layers on Sharyn's couch. Under her care, I begin to look at myself differently, learning that I am worth far more than Jake told me I was. She takes me back to the empowered frame of mind that existed before he began his abusive tirades. But even with Sharyn's support, his words are hard to forget. It's not yet automatic. Healing from this is going to be much harder than I anticipated.

My estranged husband wastes no time after our separation to begin his menacing texts and demands, sent daily at lightning speed. He sends lists of belongings he wants from the house. Every bag I deliver to the parking lot at his work entices him to make more itemized demands. When I tire of his texts and stop answering, he shifts to threats of police escorts to collect his things, but I don't care anymore. *Fuck it. Let the entire police force show up here. I don't give a damn*, I think. *I don't care what he threatens.*

Within days of Jake's departure, Dylan moves back to his home-town to live with a long-time mentor who had supported him through the years. It was a sad goodbye for Dylan and me. While we had a few parental bumps in the road, we had developed a nice relationship. I will miss that young man.

The time has come for me to put my house back in order. After I purge Jake's belongings, my closet looks like a women's boutique once again. I work into the wee hours of the night, filling trash bags with his clothing and dragging them to the basement for his next delivery demand. Every day thereafter, I slowly peel away one layer of him at a time from a bedroom and a house that have been infected for too long. It feels safe to have my bedroom back to myself, yet I can't help but wonder if there are still a few existing cameras I haven't found. The likelihood that he may be watching me from afar gives me the chills.

I climb a ladder to the top shelves in the master closet, pushing the last of his clothing from the top shelf to the floor below, watch-ing each piece fall into one heaping pile. Climbing down the ladder, I bag the clothes, but the last item catches my eye. It's a large black sweater dress.

Is this mine? Where did this come from? I don't remember ever owning a dress like this. It's much too big to be mine. The label reads XXXL.

Talking to myself, as I often do nowadays, I say, "So, in addition to all his other ghastly characteristics, I guess he cheated on me too. With a curvy woman, for sure."

I place the dress in the bag, putting the thought out of my mind. Two hours later, as I lie in bed, trying to sleep, something crosses my mind. Recently, I've had a few private conversations with acquaintances who know Jake well. Each of them has voiced their suspicions that he might be "sexually complicated." Jumping out of bed, I go back to the trash bag, rip it apart, and dig out the dress. Slipping it over my head, I gaze at myself in the full-length mirror. The dress is made of a woven fabric, well-worn and pilled, stretched in all the wrong places. The armholes are much too big for a woman's body, even for a larger woman. It is tight in the chest, certainly too small for a woman who would wear an XXXL dress. The stomach area is stretched, a perfect fit for his barrel-chested body type. The length is awkward, longer than it should be. Something just seems so odd about this garment; the design is more fitting to a large man's body than a woman's.

Pulling my arms out of the dress, I twist it around, so I can see the label on the collar. When I look online for the brand name, I find it on my first try—a manufacturer of transgender clothing.

I whisper to myself, "Dear God, Jake wears women's clothing?" *The burly, gruff guy who ridicules gay people and those with special needs is a cross-dresser?* For some strange reason, I'm not angry. I'm not surprised. Nothing rattles me anymore.

Back in bed, I envision him dressed up and walking around as the woman of the house when I'm out of town. Oh, if only Riley and Bella could talk! I am learning that there is a lot about this man I don't know. But what would I do with the answers at this point? Impulsively, despite it being one o'clock in the morning, I pick up my cell phone and press his name. I know my soon-to-be ex will not take my call. For what I have to say, voicemail will be better anyway.

"Hey, Jake, it's your wife. I'm cleaning out your things, and I just found your dress. You know, the black sweater dress you kept hidden on the top shelf of the closet? The old dress looks worn and a perfect fit for you. It looks like you've been wearing it for years. I finally know the truth, and I'm so glad to find one more reason to run from you."

I use that phone call to speak to him without fear of retribution, putting his back against the wall instead of mine. Feeling empowered,

I want him to know that I know. I'm turning the tables on an abusive man, hoping to silence him with his own dose of shame. I am not the least bit worried about his reaction or any consequence that might come my way.

His harassment stops after my voicemail. He goes silent for days, and I have no regret for causing him angst. However, after that phone call, I decide to aim higher moving forward. I don't want a lot of back and forth with him. I don't want to see or talk to him. What I do want is a quick end date to the marriage. I want to get this thing done. Going out like a lion serves no purpose for me, for it is next to impossible to sustain such anger without destroying myself along the way. I aspire to go out with quiet force, the best weapon to use against a man who doesn't understand the concept. But I must say, leaving that voicemail was extremely gratifying for me!

For the third time in one evening, I shut off the light and stare at the ceiling, eyes wide open. Every day since my separation, it seems, has been an emotionally hectic one, with me ending up in a mild state of shock at the end of it. Today I learned I have a cross-dressing estranged husband.

Chapter 25
Thanksgiving 2014

ONCE THE MOMENTUM OF the separation is in motion, I see no reason to slow the divorce process just because the holidays are upon us, although there are moments I hesitate and even acquiesce briefly before coming to my senses. I'm recovering a bit each day and becoming better able to realign myself to stay the course.

I decided earlier in the week that I was forfeiting Thanksgiving this year. Over the years, my kids' Thanksgiving tradition has been to spend the holiday with their dad, so at least they will enjoy it. I have no husband, no kids, and no energy to visit my local family. I'm not good company with all this doom and gloom going on around me anyway. Oh, well, the only person who is odd man out today is me, and I'm okay with that.

I wake up in the morning with a lonely pit in my stomach, making breakfast and appetizers for my kids, knowing they will soon head to their dad's house for dinner. Later this morning it will be only the dogs and me—such an odd feeling. I'm not sure what to do with myself. Do I sit in a corner and be distressed about a holiday missed? Or do I pick myself up and get on with the day?

I'm not sure how everyone else handles this situation but I decide that a hike on Riley Hill is a great way to stay occupied. At this time of year, I try to utilize every hiking opportunity, before the snow-covered trails force the dogs and me indoors for the winter months. The rattle of their collars wakes Riley and Bella from a sound sleep. They wag their tails feverishly, unable to contain their excitement. I tighten the laces of my hiking boots, dig out my winter hiking jacket for the first time this season, put on the dogs' collars, and step into the backyard to greet the brisk November afternoon.

Even though Riley Hill is only a block away, I dread walking through my neighborhood. Still drenched in dismay over the late-night police visits to my house, I make it a point to keep my head down and my hood on. Thankfully, it looks like I'm the only one on the street today. The dogs pull eagerly on their leashes as we make our way to Riley Hill.

Bella has been leashed since joining our family, because she arrived untrained. Even with a torn ACL and bandaged leg, she was a flight risk from the beginning, escaping every time someone opened the door. I spent weeks chasing her in my car when I first fostered her, amazed at how far she could run on three legs. I couldn't help but think, *Where are you running to? Are you trying to get home?* She's a strong-willed dog and has been a challenge to train, but she's so lovable and silly that it's hard for me not to laugh during our daily training sessions. She has worked hard to please me.

Thanksgiving Day seems like the perfect time to let Bella off leash for a trial run after months of training. I'm not optimistic, but I decide there's no better time than the present. Today is Bella's day to shine!

At the bottom of the hill, I unsnap both of their leashes, praying I won't have to chase Bella through the woods. At fifty-five pounds, Riley is well trained. Surging from a dead stop to his peak speed in seconds, as if he's gliding on air, he's a threat to his favorite prey: squirrels, mice, and the occasional rabbit. He chases deer too, but they just taunt him, letting him think he is getting close only to disappear into the woods, leaving him completely confused.

Bella is a bit overweight at eighty pounds. Her torn ACL, now healed, still slows her and has a tendency to throw her off balance.

Today, she is surprised to be free of her leash. I make a congratulatory announcement of her newfound freedom: "You're free, Bella!" Instead of running, Bella stands still, unsure of what to do next. She gazes at me in confusion. Her ears are pushed so far forward that they almost cover her eyes. She appears to be afraid, as she nudges me with her nose for reassurance. With each step I take, she pushes her head deeper against me, almost knocking me over.

"Go on now, Bella. I won't leave you. I promise," I say, as I lead her toward the path. I pat her head and use her favorite treats to coax her along, but she runs only until she catches up to me, burrowing her head between my knees and pressing against me once more.

She's afraid of something, just as I am, I think. I leave her leash off, and Bella and I walk slowly together, strolling up the hill to the open farmland, where I sit in the grass, hugging and playing with her, coaxing her to follow Riley's lead. This isn't at all what I expected; I'd thought she would run for the hills, but she doesn't. She insists I stay with her.

Every so often Riley returns to us, checking in to make sure he's not missing any hugs or treats. Suddenly, Bella begins to trot, glancing behind her to make sure I'm following. She is more concerned about where I am than where she is going. She trots a little faster and then, at her best full-speed waddle, runs to catch up with Riley.

On my first whistle, Bella returns to me with happiness spread throughout her face, satisfied with her own obedience. She lavishes in the glory, as I cover her in kisses. Filled with excitement, Bella runs to catch up with Riley, trotting together, side by side for the first time. It is a wonderful sight to behold!

The field grass has been cut for the final time this season, and the hay bales are tied and ready for gathering. A few species of birds remain, singing in the November breeze, and the bee colonies have taken shelter in their wooden apiaries. I've tried to capture the beauty of this place every season with my camera, but a photograph doesn't do it justice. It's the type of place you have to experience firsthand.

Atop the hill, I scan the neighborhoods below. I get the sense that everyone is seated at a Thanksgiving table with family who have gathered together to reminisce and dine in tradition—everyone except us. Although feeling a bit melancholy today, I am enjoying this solo holiday under a cloudless blue sky, surrounded by the farmland, together with my dogs on Riley Hill.

I run in circles with them as they jump and dance around me, begging for the last of the dog treats. I'm happy in this spot. At this juncture, I don't feel alone, despite the status of my separation or my lack of family on this holiday.

I lean back against the stone wall, looking up toward the sky. I feel a renewed sense of purpose as the dogs rest next to me, drinking bottled water from the palm of my hand. *I am thankful today*, I think. *I am thankful for my two loyal companions and for my kids. And most of all, I am thankful for my newfound freedom.*

I head back home, feeling rejuvenated and grateful. I don't foresee spending another Thanksgiving like this, but I will always fondly remember this solo holiday, a transitional Thanksgiving with the three amigos.

Chapter 26
December 2014

IT'S BEEN ALMOST A month since the separation, and I've accomplished a lot in these last few weeks. The dust seems to be settling, but the good and the bad memories plague me.

Lately I tend to focus on the good times of our marriage, even though most activities we did together, which once seemed like such fun, eventually become stressful. An experienced hiker, Jake was skilled enough to lead our hikes or our paddles down the river, but as happiness in our marriage waned, I was overcome with a sense of uncertainty when we went too deep into the woods or found ourselves in a secluded area on the river. Eventually, I stopped hiking and kayaking with him altogether, to avoid the chill that formed on the back of my neck in those remote locations.

My uncertainty wasn't brought about by being too deep in nature. It was because of the underlying aversion I had when I was alone with him. Given what I learned after our separation, I can see that my intuition was spot on.

"You dodged a bullet," a friend says, when I finally confide in her about my marriage. Truer words have never been spoken.

Yet I find myself waking in the middle of the night in tears, feeling remorse for not trying harder to fix him. To fix us. For some reason, his softer side seems to be branded in my memory. What the hell is wrong with me? Thankfully, daylight brings logic back to my divorce strategy. My goal is to have Jake served with divorce papers before Christmas, to secure a court date to finalize the end of us. It would be a Christmas present to me. But Jake has different plans. He wants to hit the pause button. Despite his bad-boy persona, he hides when the constable knocks on his apartment door to serve him divorce papers, and he refuses to return the constable's voicemails for weeks. Jake is a man on the run, and he stays on the run for two months. Only when I send the constable to his office, does Jake come out of hiding, finally accepting the fact that this process is going to happen no matter how far he runs.

Being served sends Jake into retaliation mode. His threats become more graphic by the day; he boasts about handguns and automatic weapons he would like to use to make his "problem" go away. He makes the effort to show he has the ability and frame of mind to take this divorce to a more dangerous level.

Well-meaning friends tell me, "Aw, don't worry. He's just full of hot air. He would never actually hurt you." I don't believe that to be true. I've seen things from him that other people haven't. I've seen firsthand the damage he can do, and I have no doubt he has the capability to live up to the threats he makes.

I respond to my friend's consoling words, "It's not personal until the threats are aimed at you. Then it becomes serious and life-threatening. Especially if you were to receive daily reminders from him that prove he is not in a healthy frame of mind, and somehow, it's all your fault."

The threats via text and voicemail leave me no choice but to take the next step. For the first time in months, I feel as though I have the law on my side to protect me. After weeks of advice from the Larington police lieutenant, I head to court to file a restraining order against my estranged husband.

The Massachusetts District Court issues my first restraining order against Jake in January 2014. In February, after a hearing, the court will extend the restraining order for one year. The contents of the protective order are precise. The question is, will he abide by the law or walk right through the order?

- You are ordered not to abuse the Plaintiff by harming, threatening, or attempting to harm the Plaintiff physically or by placing the Plaintiff in fear of imminent serious physical harm.

- You are ordered not to contact the Plaintiff in writing, electronically, or otherwise, either directly or through someone else, and stay at least 100 yards away from the Plaintiff.

Finally, I feel safe.

Chapter 27
February 2015

THERE IS ONLY ONE way to dress on this bitterly cold morning, and that's in my most comfortable sweats and an old fleece sweater, the kind I'll never throw away, no matter how tattered it is. Riley and Bella are curled under the desk at my feet just a few feet from the glowing fireplace. The warmth of their bodies is like a comfy pair of slippers as the wind whips past my office window. Being able to stay inside on a day like this is just one of the perks of working from home. I have a busy administrative day ahead with a pile of paperwork to generate for my clients and a list of divorce items to attend to.

Getting divorced is like having a temporary full-time job. The unfinished construction jobs he left behind are high on my list, but I can't tackle those alone. I put the home repairs out of my mind to focus on a simpler task, deleting his name from my online accounts and changing my passwords, because he's still accessing them and wreaking havoc from afar. I expect nothing less.

The cable bill that has haunted me almost as long as the pool dilemma, is an issue once more. Today I plan on putting this to rest once and for all. Thinking back to the last time, when the cable bill resulted in the police at my front door, I thank God that those days are over.

Throughout the course of the last two weeks I have dropped Jake's email from my cable account twice, but he keeps reappearing. I know he must be behind it. I have a hunch that he is using my password to retrieve his daily emails. The cable company confirms my belief, proving that he will do anything to avoid paying a bill, even one as small and personal as his own Wi-Fi. It is time to finish this action.

Within minutes, I have changed my password and added heavy security to the account, to make sure he is restricted permanently. I'm not sure why I didn't realize this after the last two attempts to delete him from my account, but this time around I realize I now own his email and all its contents. If I were a chess player, I would call this a checkmate!

To read or not to read his emails—that is the question! Thoughts come to mind of the abuse I endured with him and the hidden cameras that haunted Zoey and me. Without a second thought and just one click, I am in. From there, a whole new world opens before me, one I never knew existed.

On my first scroll of his emails, I see nothing out of the ordinary, but as I look closer, I detect a system. Just as I suspected, it includes a variety of porn videos, pictures, and emails. Some seem harmless, while others are more abstract. Female weightlifters engaging in group sex seem to be a favorite of his. Despite the content of the first folder, thus far nothing shocks me, with just one exception—excessive purchases of Viagra, something a wife should have the courtesy of knowing, but I never did.

The next email folder delivers the first dagger, more raw and personal, deep into my chest. It presents evidence of a long history over the years with prostitutes and escorts and includes encounters he documented through pictures and videos. This discovery totally crushes my belief that he didn't cheat. I think back to comments I made to my therapist, convinced that Jake and I were faithful to each other, certain that our only shared virtue was the fidelity in our marriage. I couldn't have been more wrong.

I scroll through a multitude of similar photographs and videos, seeing his wedding ring on his finger. His cell phone captured the dated timeline of an afternoon in Miami with a prostitute. His hand rested comfortably on her ass beneath her bikini bottom while they enjoyed cocktails. They continued to a hotel room, as he recorded her kneeling on the bed. Her large breasts swaying back and forth with each thrust from him as he stood behind her. Another video showed a threesome with a young prostitute, the scars still fresh under her breasts from new implants.

He photographed more of the same from Vegas and every other business stop throughout the country. Some pictures were taken at the time we first met and continued throughout the early romantic months of our relationship. Other photos were snapped one week before he moved in with me and others just days before we eloped.

All the loving texts he sent me while traveling on business come to mind. Those heartfelt text messages were nothing but lies. The emotional abuse I left him for is minuscule compared to what I am learning today.

The biggest surprises are the online personal ads he had, looking for sexual encounters with men. I quickly learn that these man-on-man trysts took place for years before we met, continued throughout our marriage, and intensified within days after our separation. His personal ads are desperate, looking for a male stranger willing to meet anywhere, in a cheap hotel or in the woods. It doesn't matter where or with whom.

I am appalled as I go through picture after picture, with some male partners looking too young to be consensual, offering sex with no questions asked. The responses are filled with lewd sexual needs and appeals to meet immediately.

I soon realize that our entire marriage has been a lie. Everything I thought we were, especially during the months I spent falling in love with him, was all a cheating, self-serving illusion.

Throughout the day I learn that the man I slept next to, and made love to, never had my best interests at heart. He had been hiring hookers and meeting men in the woods and hotel rooms since before we met, possibly for years. I am left to wonder if he enjoyed crawling into our bed and pressing his dirty body against mine after his sexual trysts.

His emails show that his objective was to find impersonal sexual encounters to satisfy the fire in his belly. All the while, he pretended to be the loyal husband he never was, and demanding that I be the vision of perfection, the devoted faithful wife under his careful watch.

When I peeked into his email, I thought I would find just a few scandalous details. Never did I imagine I would uncover a secret life of such deep deception and sexual addiction.

My body is stiff from reading all day. My mind—oh, my mind!— words cannot describe. I shut down my computer for the day with a completely different impression of my marriage and the life we lived together. I sit in silence, absorbed in thought about Jake, a man I did not know.

Zoey arrives home, and we begin our evening routine. I love it when she does her homework in my bed with me. There is so little time left for the two of us to be together before she, like her siblings, heads off to college. I want to enjoy every moment.

As nightfall washes over the house, I reflect on today, just another crazy day filled with disastrous revelations. It leaves me to wonder why I am so devastated now over his chronic infidelity and sexual addictions. I filed for divorce before discovering this mess, so what does it matter at this point?

After much thought, I realize that it matters to me out of principle. I was courted by him. He worked tirelessly to convince me to live with him. He proposed marriage, yet this man was never faithful or trustworthy, not even during our best days together. The discovery that I shared not a single honest moment with my husband is overwhelming.

It's ironic that Jake, who stalked me with security devices throughout the marriage, is the one who has the most to hide. How does he keep ahead of all the lies, while betraying so many people day after day? It must be a daunting task to live a secret life of such magnitude, having to constantly worry when those around him get a whiff of his trickery.

I finally climb into bed after this exhausting day, only to find that I cannot sleep. I stare at the ceiling long into the night, feeling not a single regret for finding out who my estranged husband is.

In the middle of the night, I wake in a cold sweat from convoluted nightmares I can't decipher. It is impossible to hold back the sobs that escape me in the darkness. There is no way to determine what I'm crying about. I just cry about it all.

Morning brings no relief. I rise with a sense of urgency, feeling less calm than yesterday, for this new information overwhelms me. Instead of updating my attorney, I make a different phone call—to my physician.

Chapter 28
The Doctor, February 2015

JUST ONE DAY AFTER my email discovery, I am sitting in my doctor's office, a holistic physician with a naturalistic approach to medicine. In the past, I have been irritated during my visits to see my doctor because she is always running late. It is during my visit on this day that I learn why that is.

I'm not handling the discovery of Jake's secret life well at all. My emotions are simmering just below the surface. The details are hitting me harder than I expected. I am terrified for my health, realizing too late that I've been exposed to sexually transmitted diseases (STDs) from his highly promiscuous lifestyle.

The doctor enters the room in her cheery, hurried fashion, as always, playing catch-up with her schedule. She washes her hands and reviews my chart while chatting away—until she turns to look at me. Without another word, she sits on her stool and wheels over to me, sitting face to face just inches away.

My voice cracks as I hold back the tears. Looking downward, instead of meeting her gaze, I say, "I need an exam and some bloodwork to rule out STDs." I close my eyes to mentally block out the reality of the words I had just spoken.

Seeing my obvious distress, she becomes more concerned with my state of mind than my worries about infection. "You don't look well. What's up?" she asks.

I don't know where to begin. "My joints hurt. My back and neck have been stiff for months. Each morning I have to hesitate before putting my feet on the floor to minimize the pain that shoots through the tops of my feet. I don't sleep more than one to two hours per night because I wake up with nightmares. I'm having difficulty being productive. I've been diagnosed with PTSD due to domestic abuse from my marriage. I am here to see you today because I am worried I might have contracted an STD from my husband's sexual activity outside of the marriage. I discovered yesterday that he has been with many female hookers, placed man-on-man ads, and has engaged in numerous affairs with men and women. From what I have uncovered, it appears to me that he has a sexual addiction."

She hesitates, as if unsure how to respond, and I nod.

"What happened?" she asks. "Last time I saw you, you had recently gotten married."

I reply softly, afraid that someone might overhear, "Dysfunction, dishonesty, cheating, chaos, verbal abuse, and control." My eyes well up again, as I continue. "I was intimate with him all this time, never knowing. I was completely unaware of his cheating. How could I be so unaware with something of this magnitude? I need to make sure I don't have any STDs. I don't think I'll ever be free from this. I feel so violated and stupid."

My doctor doesn't move a muscle, keeping her hands resting on my thighs. She takes a moment, as she forms her response. "You are very thin. I see from your chart that you have lost quite a bit of weight. Trauma wreaks havoc on your body, your sleep, and your ability to think clearly. You can't exist or be healthy when you sleep only two hours per night and you don't eat. You're exhausted, humiliated, sad, and angry. You're safe here. Are you safe at home?"

"No. Even though he's not living in the house, I never know what he might do. His public taunting on social media frightens me. He's far too interested in guns and other weapons. He wants to punish me with uncertainty and humiliation for leaving the marriage. I'm tired and exhausted every day from this existence."

She reviews with me the signs of chronic trauma and emotional abuse, matching most of them to my symptoms. Hearing her words comforts me enough that I stop trembling.

She asks one final question: "Do you think of hurting yourself?"

I need to gather my thoughts on this one. It will be a complicated answer. "I don't think of ending my life, but lately I do wonder about the value of this life of mine. He has told me for so long what a piece of shit I am, and it's taken its toll on me. After a lot of reflection and self-loathing, I realize that I do matter. The love for my kids and their love for me keeps me going. Our time spent together evolving as a family is the richest, most important piece of my life, and I wouldn't give up a single moment of it for anything."

I continue, "I'm not upset about the breakup of the marriage. I began to question it shortly after we married. But today I find myself blindsided by realizing too late that I married a man with such a morally corrosive lifestyle—in addition to the emotional abuse I endured with him."

Never did I imagine, even for a second, that at fifty-four years old I would be lying on an exam table with my feet in stirrups, searching for deeper violations in my marriage than I had thought possible.

My mind wanders as the exam continues. I am disposable in his eyes. How can I not be worthy of a single day of truth from the person who was my husband? Everyone tells me, "Oh, it's not you, Stella. It's him. He's the problem."

In return, I ask them, "How so? I was part of a marriage in which I allowed myself to be destroyed by a man who doesn't have the slightest idea how to love anyone other than himself."

As I lie here, the emails and the pictures I discovered the day before keep circling in my head. I see pictures of one of his girlfriends lying naked in my bed, leaning against my upholstered headboard with her overly tanned body and leathery skin, smiling at the camera as she drinks from my grandmother's wineglass. Her eyes glow with satisfaction to be invading another woman's home.

According to the email correspondence that I read, she liked to drive past my house when she was in town visiting her daughter, a boarding student at Larington Academy. She wanted to see where we lived and imagine a glorified version of how she could reside there instead of me.

As my exam goes on much longer than I expected, a December 2011 email from Jake to one of his long-term male lovers crosses my mind. Just a few months after we moved in together, Jake sent his male lover, Alan, an emotional letter, reminiscing about their past sexual encounters. He asks if they can continue their shared man-on-man trysts by adding a third partner, to which his lover eagerly agrees.

Jake takes it a step further by pursuing a deeper relationship with him. "I was going through our ads and was thinking about how fun it would be if you and I could buy a house together. Can't wait to see you next week for the home inspection." It was clear by their correspondence that Jake was pining away for him and that their sexual connection was still strong.

Jake and Alan were colleagues who had worked together in the past. Alan's response to the email was just as poignant, but he reminded Jake to be careful when they were to meet the next week, for he would be with his wife—just another oblivious wife, like me, who probably had no idea about the health risks her husband was subjecting her to. I thought many times about reaching out to her. I know her name. I sure wish someone had enlightened me. But in the end, I just couldn't do it. The last thing I wanted was to invade a stranger's marriage.

With my exam finally over, I leave with a hug from my doctor and a scolding for missing my thyroid ultrasound a month ago.

"I've been kind of busy lately," I say, "and exhausted."

She smiles and recites Ernest Hemingway: "'Courage is grace under pressure.' Let that be your mantra, Stella."

As I walk down the hall after my long, drawn-out time with the doctor, I can see patients waiting to see her. *If they only knew why she runs late all the time*, I think. A week later, she calls to deliver the news. I am free from all STDs but will need another exam in six months.

My email discovery and this invasive doctor's appointment have been an unexpected detour that has shaken my world and opened my eyes to the depth of deceit in which I lived.

Chapter 29
February 2015

I'VE MANAGED TO ESCAPE the approaching Valentine's Day by catching a last-minute flight out of town, doing whatever I can to avoid the holiday this year. While most people on this flight are traveling toward romance, I happen to be running from it. I've never been a fan of the holiday.

I'm buckled into my window seat, 8F, for this early morning flight, as the plane speeds down the runway and lifts effortlessly into the air. I'm heading toward the sunshine, with my headphones on to avoid conversation with the person seated next to me. Socializing has not been my forte lately. I avoid it at best.

I think back to how I spent Valentine's Day 2014. Jake and I had a minor disagreement a few days prior to the horrid holiday, as he was leaving for a business trip to Miami. Within hours of his arrival in Miami, pictures of him and his ringless finger began circulating, a direct message to me that he was a free man any time he wished to be. In his world, marriage was as simple as slipping the ring on and off his finger. He enjoyed the effect his drama had on me. It was his way of avenging any perceived discord between us. Prior to our marriage, when we were just roommates, I had no idea behavior like this was imminent.

Fast-forward to this year. On Valentine's Day 2015, I am separated, facing divorce, and trying to nonchalantly free myself from the divorce pressure by escaping this dreaded holiday. I stare out the window, as I drift between the clouds.

My mom awaits my arrival in Naples. Her kind heart and wisdom have been my rock through this ordeal. I can't wait to spend some downtime with the sand between my toes. I might not have romance on this holiday, but given the dysfunction I'm running from, Naples is a safe place to land and a warm place to hide for a few days.

No matter how far away I go, the disturbing thoughts still circulate. I'm sure his Southern girlfriend with the leather skin thought she was stealing away a real keeper at the time she laid her naked presence across another woman's bed, but I was the winner here. I gained my freedom while she knowingly settled for a cheating man. With that thought in mind, I turn up the volume on my headphones, as we prepare to land. Trays are up. Seatbelts are buckled. I have successfully escaped to the Sunshine State.

I step off the elevator into the apartment and get a hug from Mom. Over her shoulder, I eye the freshly made sandwich on the counter. Quickly shedding my winter clothes, I pull out whatever is within reach in my half-open suitcase, changing into baggy shorts and an old tank top. I wash the makeup and grime from my face and dive into my favorite cushioned chaise on the lanai, with the ocean view spreading out before me. It feels awesome to have my shoes and socks off and the sunbaked tile warming my feet in the middle of February. I inhale the ocean's scent and delight in the sounds from the beach crowd below, playing and swimming in the midday sun while I devour my turkey sandwich.

As the weekend passes, I begin to feel calmer. It's difficult to be dismal in this oceanside paradise. When I first arrive here, I always find it awkward to greet those who pass me on my beach walks. They all seem so happy and eager to say hello or give a friendly nod of the head. Down here, people look out at the ocean, up to the sky, and directly into your eyes when they speak to you. In the city I come from, we spend more time looking down at our cell phones and deliberately avoiding eye contact, ignoring those who walk past us.

It doesn't take me long to reacquaint myself with the Southern friendliness by offering return greetings, adding a cheery "Good morning!" to those passing my way. It's the Naples way of living on the beach, and it's contagious.

The days are spent relaxing at the beach with my chair placed close enough to the shore, so each wave barely reaches my toes. Hours pass as I people-watch, wondering what their life stories might entail. My nights are spent on the lanai watching the sunset with a glass of Chardonnay, in full appreciation of peaceful moments. These simple pleasures strum a harmony I haven't felt in so long. Simplistic is something I thought I would never experience again, yet here I am.

I'm not sure how he knows, but as I might have expected, Jake is still tracking me. It's his way of letting me know I can't escape him. He can find me anywhere. I have had to purchase a new laptop because of keystroke tracking. I still have a mechanic check my car regularly for GPS devices. I guess I'm going to have to trade in my phone. I know of no other way he could track me.

I must remember that this is a battle of perseverance, not opposition. Each day I am further away from him and one day closer to being divorced. I am strong. I am in control of my life now. His intimidation will not break me.

Far too soon, I have to return to Boston, stepping into the frigid winter air, where everyone is bundled tightly under winter coats and hats. The short getaway at the beach was well spent. I feel lighter in my step. My tanned skin under my heavy jacket is still warm from the sun.

I climb into a cab, looking forward to getting home again to Zoey and the dogs.

As many people predicted, just a few weeks into the protective order, Jake is on the cusp of violating the order, even though he's been warned to back off. In response, he fires off more threats, posting more videos about his interest in guns and large hunting knives.

He posts videos that show death to dogs. One in particular is especially upsetting, a video of a dead black Lab that resembles my beautiful Bella, in the mouth of an alligator, floating downriver. My one-acre backyard has been a refuge for my dogs. Riley and Bella sun themselves, nap in the shade of the trees and romp in the snow—but not anymore. The backyard is now off-limits. I don't let my dogs out of my sight.

Those in my village worry greatly about his callous ability to push the confines of the restraining order to the absolute limit with his vocal admiration of weapons. They believe he is capable of walking right through the order, which could result in a disastrous outcome for me. Restraining orders, guns and automatic weapons, his anger combined with hatred, and innocent dead animals consume my thoughts. Is he standing in the woods behind my house, as he often joked? These are games of intimidation executed from the mind of a psychopath. He makes it evident that, even with a protective order issued by a judge, he has no intention of going away in a refined manner.

Knowing that someone is stalking you—wishing you and your loved ones dead—is one of the most stress-inducing situations you could ever experience. There is a fear, a sense of nervousness, creating a measure of paranoia that never goes away. It lives with you forever; you cannot trust that a safe life will ever be possible.

Each time I catch a flight out of town, my eyes scan the airport, cautiously searching for his presence. I have turned my car around countless times and headed back home to recheck that I've locked my doors and windows. I pull my shades down every night. I avoid going out after dark, for I have the distinct feeling that he will resurface without notice. I am cognizant of the fact that I am not free. I am held hostage with fear and I can't seem to shake it.

I make it a point to speak up about his stalking, letting those around me know that he's still stepping over the line of decency. A private investigator I've hired assures me his behavior is well documented. Such great lengths I must take for the simple luxury of instilling the no-contact rule. At the suggestion of the Larington police department, I file for a court hearing to address a possible violation of the restraining order. I find myself sitting in a closed hearing with a court magistrate, two court officers, the Larington police lieutenant, Jake, and his attorney. I was told that attorneys were not allowed in this meeting, yet Jake is allowed to keep his attorney present.

From the start, that leaves me without counsel and the sole female in the room, trying to convince six men that my estranged husband is becoming a predator, who is violating the protective order I took out on him weeks prior. There is no psychologist present at the table and no one, to the best of my knowledge, who has qualifications related to domestic abuse.

The magistrate chooses me to speak first. I have come prepared, taking approximately ten minutes to explain why I have gathered them here for this hearing. I explain that Jake still has possession of unregistered guns, which were supposed to have been confiscated when the police served him with the restraining order, but the police never bothered to search, even though I provided the location where they were most likely stored. I show them pictures of him shooting out his son's bedroom window.

Jake has harassed me so often that I have to present my backup documentation in a three-ring notebook. This isn't the occasional dig on social media. I show them proof he is stalking me by posting pictures of places where I am traveling privately and restaurants where I am dining. I pass around his posts, wishing death for my pets, and I show them his infatuation with assault weapons, along with his outspoken hatred of me. These daily occurrences by my estranged husband while under a restraining order are extremely concerning to everyone—except the people in this room.

In the end, none of it matters. The magistrate isn't convinced, finding that, while Jake's posts and threats are concerning, he is not in violation of the restraining order, because it does not prove intent and because he posted some of them on social media rather than calling me on the phone or sending me a direct email.

"I see his attempts as ambiguous," the magistrate pronounces. "Those threats might have nothing to do with you. You can't prove they are directly related to you, even though he uses the words 'my wife' in some of them. He didn't reach out to you directly, so he's not in violation."

He then asks Jake, "Do you have any concealed weapons anywhere in your home or stored away?"

Jake answers calmly with a smile, "No."

Turning his attention back to me, the magistrate says, "Then there is nothing more we can do."

It becomes obvious to me as I sit at the table that restraining orders are not worth the paper they're written on.

During this encounter, while sitting directly across from me, Jake never turns to me to say, "I'm sorry. I didn't mean to scare you" or "I would never want you to live in fear"—because "in fear" is exactly how he intends for me to live. Instead of being remorseful, he smirks and enjoys his time in the limelight. He passes notes back and forth with his attorney, the two of them rolling their eyes when I speak, neither of them taking this seriously.

I didn't file this restraining order because I am angry. I didn't do it for revenge. I gave the matter deep thought before doing so. I filed because I live in fear of my estranged husband and the threats he so enjoys making toward me. I filed because Jake is dangerous when angry. Few know better than I how this man has cycles of abuse that are beyond dangerous, and a restraining order has not slowed him down. Yet the magistrate feels all is well with my abuser's actions.

It is difficult for a woman, or anyone who lives in fear, to go before a judge and receive a valid restraining order, only to have a roomful of men decide that her estranged husband, who is sitting directly across the table, is allowed to harass and induce enough fear that she becomes afraid to leave her home. The whole sordid handling of the hearing makes me wonder whether tonight is the night that, empowered by the magistrate's decision, he'll come to the house, drunk on wine and vodka with gun in hand, knowing he can blur the lines of a restraining order without repercussions.

I'm sure that if the people in that meeting had the opportunity to speak on this today, they would still claim it was handled fairly, but I have no doubt that if it had been one of their daughters sitting in my seat, the outcome would have been vastly different.

Today, no one at the magistrate's table questions Jake's lack of remorse or wonders where his guns might be. They refuse to perform due diligence pertaining to his firearms, even though I provided proof and a roadmap for the police to follow. The magistrate seems far more concerned with the risk of litigation if they touch on his civil rights than with protecting mine. I've never felt more vulnerable, and I have the distinct feeling I am lost in the good ol' boy network.

After the magistrate hands down his decision, Jake and his attorney leave the courthouse smiling, patting each other on the back. With the room empty, the magistrate makes an attempt to deliver a half-assed apology to me, telling me that the East Coast courts are "somewhat behind the times in regard to social media, texting, and restraining orders." I just look at him with a long silence.

Inside, my brain is smoking. *Gee, thanks, asshole. Next time, grow some balls and do the right thing.*

One would think that at the end of such a hearing pertaining to restraining orders, the magistrate would have enough training regarding these situations to retain Jake, allowing me time to exit and walk safely to my car first, just as the judges do when restraining orders are issued. After all, I am the one who took out the restraining order, and I am the one who filed the complaint that resulted in today's meeting.

Instead, the magistrate just dismisses us both at the same time. It never dawns on him to ensure a safe exit, even after hearing Jake's history.

So, feeling both furious and powerless, I take it upon myself to wait in the corner of the room as the magistrate moves on to another case. I am left to wonder whether Jake will live up to his threats by waiting patiently for me in the parking garage across the street from the courthouse. Even after waiting for over fifteen minutes, I am too scared to walk to my car alone. Finally, I ask the Larington police lieutenant who was seated next to me at the hearing to escort me to my car.

I know the magistrate and his cronies didn't see it, but I faced fear in that meeting. I faced my abuser and looked him straight in the eye—but the bully didn't even get a slap on the wrist. I doubt any of the men in that meeting have been threatened and harassed repeatedly by a psychopath who has no respect for lawful boundaries and who is far bigger and more physically powerful than they are.

I now understand why women don't come forward to speak out about domestic abuse. First, in my case, the men at the table were disinterested, and it only antagonized my abuser more, placing me at greater risk. Second, when I did come forward, the lines within the restraining order proved so gray that it was next to impossible to prove a violation. This is called "living in fear," gentlemen, and no one should have to live like this.

At this point, even uttering his name is difficult. I find it much easier to call him by the nickname I gave him upon our separation. And so, without further ado, his name is changed in my world.

"Hello, Dick."

Those who are privy to the situation agree it to be a suitable name for him.

After my unsuccessful meeting with the court, I decide the time has come for me to have a different focus. The courts refuse to help me, and the police are unable to. They have no interest in me unless I am a corpse. I need to help myself.

From that point forward, I make Dick a part of my past and refuse to include him in my present, despite his daily efforts to reach me in some destructive manner. I must be finished with it, or it will finish me. Regardless of my experience with the magistrate earlier in the week, I set my sights on rediscovering my own power. I dig out the Mace I carried with me when I hiked, keeping one can of it in my nightstand drawer and another in my purse, ready to spray deep into his eyes if he comes close to me. If need be, I'll blind him.

I have decided it's time for me to tell a different story now. I have a new morning mantra: "I am not a victim; I am a survivor. Only I define who I am. I am courageous. I am worthy. I am determined." I think back to what has made me feel empowered in the past, and the first thing that comes to mind is yoga.

The next day I unroll my mat in the back corner of the yoga studio for a 6:00 a.m. vinyasa class. Within the four corners of my mat, I turn inward. It is a practice of the humble warrior, as I struggle to assume the most basic positions that used to be so easy. My flow is choppy and unbalanced. My flexibility is minimal, and my joints scream in pain. Regardless, I concentrate on my yoga breath, feeling gratitude for being on my mat in this warm, dark studio on a frosty winter morning.

After a few weeks of daily practice, my legs begin to carry me freely through the flow. I enjoy the challenge and the physical heat I feel. My underweight, malnourished body is showing signs of oxygenation. The reflection in the mirror shows improvement in my posture, as I stand fully balanced in a tree pose. These changes in my physique might seem minuscule to some, but I am grateful for the gradual progression, especially the ability to breathe deeply without sharp pain in my lungs.

I return to my organic eating, craving healthy food and putting nutrients back into this body of mine. Chocolate chip cookie dinners during a psychopathic divorce can sustain you for only so long. My shoulders are now showing more definition. I no longer slump forward.

Instead I stand taller. My mind is clearing. This warrior is rising, slowly but surely.

I walk alone during this time in my life, but I don't feel alone. *I am enough.* I don't need the courts. I have my mat, whereupon I find peace and growth. I have my children, my home, and my dogs. I have myself.

The upside to sweating profusely through hot yoga is the pleasure of a deep meditation. After an hour-long practice, my body is limber and strong. It is time for savasana, the final resting posture. The class falls into child's pose with a strong breath out to release inner heat built during the practice. A simple exhalation seems like such a reward after this difficult class. The room darkens; the music softens. I lie on my mat, feeling at peace. I am covered in sweat, yet warm without a chill. It's heaven on earth.

Meditation seeps in. I envision living in peace with a comfortable flow to my life. My children and I have traveled to different places these past few years, and we are each learning more about ourselves. I see a day when we return to spending family time together once more, adding new members to our tribe of four.

The instructor gently adjusts my neck, rubbing peppermint oil on my shoulders with her firm hands as the savasana draws to a gradual close, taking me to a glorious state of radiance. It is 7:00 a.m., and I am ready to start my day. I leave the studio in a meditative trance, feeling peaceful.

Hello, tranquility. It's been too long. Welcome home. Namaste.

Chapter 30
The Night Sky, March 2015

UPON MY ARRIVAL AT each therapy session, Sharyn waits for me in her chair. With a look of concern and bated breath, she always asks cautiously, "How are you? What happened this week? Are you okay?" Her questions make me smile for two reasons. First, it is nice to know that someone is thinking of me, while I'm on the front lines of divorce from a psychopath. Second, it shows me that even my therapist views this divorce as more dangerous than most. In fact, she has issued that warning to me on many occasions. I can tell by her questions and the details she pulls from my stories that she is concerned for my safety, as it pertains to this man.

I rely heavily on these sessions with Sharyn. She knows every sordid detail of this voyage, the dark days and my layers of recovery. I often arrive at her office disheveled, in shock, in anguish, and sometimes in tears. I am afraid—very much afraid of his intimidation. I am distressed at the thought of losing everything in a divorce settlement. It is here, on Sharyn's couch, where I release the stress, exposing my pain. And the pain is deep; it's deeper than anything I have ever experienced in my lifetime.

The verbal and emotional abuse was the reason for my decision to end the marriage. I had lived with it and fought hard against it. Yet at this point in my therapy, it is more like a scar than an open wound. Since I filed for divorce in December, it is the endless intimidation, the threats, and the discovery of his deep-rooted deceit and his sexual addictions that are now front and center.

I understand fully that this discovery came about because I peeked behind the curtain of his emails. Some might say I brought it on myself. But, after being victimized on so many levels by him, I feel I owed the discovery to myself, especially since the opportunity to dig deeper dropped into my lap. I have absolutely no regrets for finding out who my husband was within our marriage. The pain I go through now, while difficult, is an awakening to the truth I deserve to know.

The discussions between Sharyn and me are expansive. They run the gamut from childhood, to marriage, my siblings, parenting, regret, my hopes, and of course this crazy divorce. I learned early on that Sharyn is a strength builder. She bolsters my resolve. I might have to return to her multiple times a week for further guidance, but her message of strength is always there for me to access.

The most important component of her guidance is this: "When this is over, and you've left the darkness behind, what will you do with the new light? Will you repeat this mistake, only to stumble upon another abusive connection, as many do? Or will you be different? Will you know yourself better? Will you put yourself first? Will you speak up? Will you have strong boundaries?" It is here where her lesson and strength-building lie.

Sharyn often circles back to a specific line of questioning: "Where is it that you encounter the most difficulty?"

I reply with the simple answer I know to be true: "Shame is a heavy burden to bear, Sharyn. Shame is the hardest thing of all to lift from my shoulders, and it has been there for as long as I can remember."

Her follow-up question points me back toward the positive: "What strengths do you consider to be your most prominent virtue?"

"I have a strong faith in the quality of my inner self. I learned at an early age that I am brave." Both these affirmations have been a steady presence in me for as long as I can remember, until I faced the wrath of Jake. "Whether they were taken from me or I gave them away, I want those virtues back. They belong to me."

Since my separation, I have returned to my childhood roots by seeking refuge within myself. Being more of an introvert, I take this time to reinforce my intentions daily and to study my favorite philosophers and spiritual healers.

With the dogs by my side and the fireplace roaring, I read in my spare time and listen to audios that interest me, absorbing the words and teachings of Dr. Wayne Dyer, Esther and Jerry Hicks, Deepak Chopra, David Hawkins, the Dalai Lama, and Gangaji. Their metaphysical influence and their calming effect mesmerize me, bringing peace to my erratic slumber.

Using the power of prayer, I ask daily for acceptance and guidance in the days ahead. Sometimes I pray just to say, "Today was a good day. Thank you, Lord."

Other days, especially in recent months, I search for a sign that the Lord has not bypassed me and that he sees me, loves me, and is present during the difficult times. I don't ask to be removed from the dark path, only that he light the way. Other times, I need nothing more than a sunny day to recognize the spirit in everything I see and do. I often think the Lord must be so amused by us humans, a chaotic bunch of beings who have such difficulty realizing that all we desire rests at our fingertips.

The "law of attraction" is the guiding principle that helps me to strengthen the power of "I am." *I am enough.* My studies are not based on religion, nor is it practiced through preaching. It is practiced within; offering a take-what-you-need-and-leave-the-rest philosophy. It teaches you to pursue enlightenment through your thoughts. Nothing is unattainable if you truly want it. I have found so many ways to be touched each day by one or more of these resources.

This winter has been long and dark, with snowfalls reaching record proportions, but the sky has been spectacular lately, making up for the plummeting temperatures.

Tonight is brighter than most, with a sky full of stars. I stand at the back door of my house every evening with the dogs to give thanks, but tonight, for some reason, this miraculous view strikes me differently. The brilliance of one particular star catches my attention, and I can't take my eyes off it, tracing its light to the ground.

Standing on the threshold of the door to keep warm, I say out loud with a smile, "Is that you, Dad? I hope you are soaring, wherever you are! Thank you for watching over me. I love you."

Calling the dogs back in, I lock the door and prepare for bed, but I can't stop thinking about the expansive sky. Without a second thought, I pull on my sweatpants and go back to the door, sliding it open wide.

Bella follows me from the bedroom, settling comfortably behind me with her front paws crossed, claiming her front-row seat alongside me at the back door. The star is still there, shining in all its glory and lighting up the ice-clad branches in the surrounding woods.

I stand on the patio, wanting to get closer to the line of light. I can feel the freezing temperature seeping into my bare feet, as I step onto the stone. The winter chill ripples through my T-shirt and onto my skin. I'm not sure how long I stand there on the bluestone patio, but I feel no discomfort. I am so peaceful here under this illuminated sky tonight. The brilliance of the universe amazes me. I've stood here so many times over the years and have never felt it so tranquil. After a period of time, I sense a slow, subtle shift, a lifting of energy from inside me. There is a feeling of warmth inside my body, but on the outside my skin is still cool.

I crouch to sit on the low step, my knees pulled tightly to my chest, with my arms wrapped around my shins. This warm energy continues to

CHAPTER 30

flow through me, bringing me to an emotional stillness. I sit quietly, not wanting anything to change, just appreciating a moment of pure peace.

I sigh out loud, the vapor of my breath turning into condensation in the freezing night air. Forthwith, I feel a sorrow like I've never felt before; it's coming from the same place in my body where I had, just seconds ago, felt a comforting warmth. My back straightens toward the sky, and, without knowing why, I pray for forgiveness.

I ask for mercy for feeling so contrite, making mistakes, turning a blind eye when I was falling in love, letting my kids down, for tarnishing my reputation with this failed marriage, allowing my boundaries to become blurred, and for hiding behind my shame for so many years. My head is hung low, resting on my knees, as I curl in tighter on the step, the cold breeze blowing the thin strands of hair on the back of my neck.

The only warmth is Bella's breath on my lower back, but I still feel no chill. Sobs take flight from inside me, from the remote place where consciousness resides. My gut clenches so hard that it feels like steel, burning from a tightness that I can't release. As I exhale deeply, the pain in my stomach dissipates, releasing the tension in my back that I've been unable to shed for over a year.

"I'll do anything," I say to the universe, through my sobs and running nose. "Please, help me to heal, God. Not just from the here and now, but from it all.

Feeling a presence, I say, "Dad, I know you're here. I can't bring myself back to life, and I'm afraid. I need some guidance. Please help me to forgive myself. I'm trying. I'm failing terribly."

I have no tissues, just the hem of my T-shirt to wipe my nose and tear-stained face. The sobs continue from deep within me with no end in sight.

After what feels like forever, I feel a slow expansion of love so deep that it overwhelms me. It's a dual feeling—I sense anguish and, at the same time, the unmistakable presence of God's unconditional love.

Without knowing why, I offer my whole self to the stars, out of pure exhaustion. "Take from me whatever you wish," I say. "Please help me to heal. Show me what I need to do. I want to trust in myself again. I am blind on this path of mine."

Here on this cold winter night, I am brought back to my core beliefs on faith and revival. This is not a moment of biblical insight or physical healing, of that I am sure, but rather a spiritual cleansing of sorts. I want so badly to continue with a new love for myself and it is clear that the time of renewal has arrived. I feel resistance draining from me and in its place is a definitive presence of comfort.

With each deep breath, I inhale the blessing of the moment, brimming with a newfound sense of purpose. Each breath feels like a loving acceptance of what is to be, leaving me humbled and physically drained. The dreaded fear that has been ringing in my ears for so long has vanished.

My eyes are still fixated on the star that drew me back outside on this wintry night. I am eternally grateful that I followed its lead, but I did so with no expectation other than to see the beauty of a winter sky. In return, I received the greatest gift of all, a cleansing. In its place, I have peace within.

Time has no value in this moment. After what seems like a lifetime has passed—and perhaps my old life did—my awareness returns. But I don't want to leave this spot, where I feel such a connection and a humbling sense of devotion. I don't want the light of the universe to diminish upon the rising of a new day. I want to remain here forever in the space, feeling the strength of this surreal affinity that the universe has just bestowed on me. I have been truly blessed.

I don't care about being outdoors during the winter freeze. Instead, I wish I could stay here forever, but I force myself to rise from the steps. The chilling temperature penetrates my bare feet for the first time. I return to the house feeling divine, knowing I will never forget this night.

Bella refuses to come to bed, choosing instead to sleep inside by the back door, looking out into the night sky. I wish I could sleep by the door with her.

Finally returning to bed, my feet and hands unusually warm, I turn off the light with a quick glance at the clock: 2:15 a.m. I spent two hours outside with no shoes or jacket in the middle of winter, yet I feel no chill.

I wake in the night to throw the heavier blankets off me because I am so warm. I sleep soundly through the night and wake in the morning with a sacred knowledge that I can move mountains.

The next day, I am eager for evening to come, but as beautiful as the night sky is, the light has moved on. I see its absence as a good thing. All I can hope for is that tonight some other distressed soul who is too close to the edge will look to the sky to receive its deliverance during his or her time of need, to experience the truest of blessings.

From that night forward, my nightmares diminish and eventually disappear.

Chapter 31
March 2015

I WAKE UP EARLY on this first Monday in March, feeling an emotional thaw in my bones, ready for my morning meditation. A light snowfall has made everything outside my window look clean. I sit on the warm, hardwood floor directly in the path of the day's first ray of sun, which warms me far better than the dry heat that's been pumping through the vents all winter long. I can feel things are getting better for me in this odd divorce. I am closer to the end. My thoughts are more fluid these days, and my outlook is more positive. My village is strong.

I slip into deep thought, recognizing that I like myself. As a matter of fact, I love who I am and what I stand for. I've reached a point in my meditation where I'm not sure exactly what happens when I drift off, but I know that I wake with a serenity like no other. As I enter back into reality, I silently celebrate the fact I'm no longer in survival mode. My legs have stopped twitching, and my hands aren't shaking constantly. I haven't needed an aspirin for muscle pain since my exchange on the patio under the night sky. I'm sure my mother is thrilled to no longer be on call as the hotline counselor for my daily crisis phone calls. Each day after meditation I drift a bit closer to true peace. By eight o'clock, I am showered and at my desk, ready for a productive day.

At quarter after eight, my first call of the day comes in. It's an unrecognizable number. *Should I pass or answer?* Feeling energetic, I decide to answer, and Dr. Reynolds, my endocrinologist, greets me. After some nudging from my doctor, I had finally gotten the overdue biopsy she had ordered months earlier and had forgotten about this expected call from him. The day so far has been good, and I have no doubt this phone call will end on a positive note.

I listen carefully as he tells me the news. The biopsy is positive for a possible malignant growth on my thyroid. While one nodule was the focus, the test found a second nodule that might have the same outcome.

I interrupt him with my first question. "So, are you saying I have thyroid cancer?"

He hesitates and then says, "Yes, we do believe you have an 85 percent chance, yet it's something we can take care of with surgery. We are confident that we have caught yours early enough."

The news hits me like a brick. *I have thyroid cancer.* I haven't given it any thought since the biopsy last week, convinced I was going to be fine. The term *cancer* sends my stomach to my toes.

Dr. Reynolds continues with the conversation in a matter-of-fact way, summarizing the prognosis, the surgery, and recovery, as I try to keep my composure. I hear him recommending surgical options and giving me the names of surgeons within his department, but I can't comprehend much of what he's saying except for the recurring word *cancer*.

As if from a distance, I hear him ask me, "Do you have a preference for any of the surgeons I just mentioned?"

In my mind, I'm screaming, "Just send me to the best doctor you've got and get this cancer out of my neck!" but out of my mouth comes, "Please send me their names, so I can do some research before deciding." All I want at this moment is to hang up as quickly as possible and have my own private breakdown. The phone call ends with the same pleasantries it started with, leaving me to wonder how many of those calls he'll make today.

With Zoey at school, the house is quiet. I can hear the heat clicking on and off throughout the house. I'm numb, not realizing I've been sitting at my desk in silence, staring into my office fireplace, as the last log burns into ash. I look over at my dogs lying in their dog beds, staring at me and measuring my silent inaction.

I wonder how much Riley and Bella perceive human emotion. They must be so tired of seeing me sad. In their dog minds, they must look at each other and think, *Oh, boy! Here she goes again!* They surely know something is happening this morning, and they won't budge until they receive a command from me.

Riley, Bella, and I, the three amigos, sit together on our white shag rug, recovering from another curveball. I am counting the hours until Zoey comes home from school. I need to pull myself together before then. She needs to see strength, not her mother sitting on the floor holding on to her dogs.

An hour passes, and I've spent it at my computer, keeping the cancer news to myself for a bit longer. There are no questions to answer, no decisions to make, no advice to hear, or no sob stories to tell. It's just my own thoughts for now. A new fear grows in my chest, as my mind races with worry. *What if I get really sick? What if I need radiation or chemo? What will my kids do without me if I die? What will become of me? Who will take care of me if I become ill? How will I get divorced as quickly as I had planned? What if I die and I'm still married to Dick?*

After having a lengthy discussion with myself, I decide to research online about my prognosis—a big mistake. Now I discover the worst about thyroid cancer, causing the fear to run alongside me, doing everything in its power to push me over the edge. I envision that I have one foot in the grave while Dick moves back into my house with his girlfriend, who has been itching to live my life.

Then, with a strange sense of calm, I decide to march forward. It's a frustrating and challenging affirmation. It's another relay race to run, this time with cancer, when I haven't even finished the divorce lap. I'm growing weary of facing these difficult decisions by myself. But for now, I'm facing it alone, and I have to be okay with that.

I've had enough time to digest my cancer diagnosis from this morning. Just when my mom thought it was safe to put her cell phone away, I am dialing her number once more.

As soon as she answers, I break the news with just one sentence: "Mom, the doctor thinks I have thyroid cancer."

Through the dead silence, I can hear her sigh heavily, trying to calm herself. She's smart enough to know that only one of us at a time should have a meltdown, and, clearly, it's still my turn.

She listens and cries, reassuring me, "I'm here for you, and I love you. I don't care what it takes. You know you can beat this, and you know we will do anything to make sure you get well."

For the first time since receiving the news this morning, I begin to weep—about cancer, and my never-ending exhaustion. She stays quiet and listens, and then she listens some more until I'm calm enough to hear her words of comfort. My mom, I love her so.

Zoey arrives home with her usual flair, but I don't have the courage to tell her the news yet. I'm not settled with it myself, and I need to be strong when I tell her. The time will come, but I doubt it will be tonight. I make her favorite meal—breakfast for dinner of cinnamon French toast, warm syrup, and bananas. We sit in our kitchen, chatting and eating, when it dawns on me for the hundredth time that life together with my children is dwindling much too quickly and there isn't a damn thing I can do about it. Then, out of the blue, I say, "I got some weird news today. My doctor says I should have my thyroid removed 'cause I might have cancer. But it will be okay. It's just some surgery."

Zoey looks at me for a brief moment, gives me her infamous wink, and says, "Well, I'll still like you even if you don't have a thyroid. Can I have the last piece of French toast?" I smile in amazement at her ease and ability to lessen my worry. Enough said.

I call Harris and Julia before bed to break the news. My delivery is the same as it was with Zoey. "No worries, everything will be fine. I'll keep you posted." I go to bed and stare at the ceiling once more, feeling very much alone but loved greatly by my children.

With no one beside me at 2:00 a.m. to console me, anxiety rudely awakens me, ready to instill more uncertainty into my gut before sunrise. I examine everything that could go wrong with the surgery and my recovery. The sun slowly rises. I am weary but ready to face another day. The light of dawn continues to be my saving grace.

Within three weeks of my diagnosis, I've been poked and prodded, and finally I'm sitting with my surgeon in a pre-op appointment, as he explains the step-by-step surgical procedure. At this point, I'm resolute about the cancer—out of necessity, not by choice. I spend the following days tidying the house and finishing loose ends with clients. I look at everything as if I'll never return home, due to my pending death under the knife.

As usual, Zoey doesn't console me but does her best to make me laugh. I can see she's nervous too. It's just the two of us here, after all.

A few days later, we head into Boston for my 5:00 a.m. surgery drop-off. For the first few minutes of our ride, Zoey's focus is on her early awakening.

"Really? It's five in the morning, Mom. Who operates on a person so early? It can't be safe. If I were a doctor, I wouldn't start my surgeries until at least noon."

"Yes, Zoey, I have no doubt," I say. "Why not just make it one o'clock, so you can fit lunch in beforehand?"

"Even better!", she says with a smile.

The commute into Boston is lovely at sunrise, especially with no traffic. Zoey and I carry on with our usual banter, her humor helping my nerves. As Zoey drops me at the front door of the hospital, she lingers a few moments longer than usual and says, "Love you, Mom."

"I love you too, Zoey." I close the car door and head off to surgery.

I don't usually feel alone when I'm by myself, but today I'm feeling it deeply. For a brief moment, I selfishly regret my decision to do this without my kids' involvement. But in my next breath, I realize this was the right decision. The last thing I want is for any of my kids to see me hooked up to machines and looking vulnerable.

As I enter pre-op, I'm amazed how crowded it is. It's so early in the morning. Administrators herd surgical patients through the healthcare insurance and payment process like cattle.

There's not a seat to be found in the waiting room. Everyone seems to have someone by their side to help with the medical forms, to hold hands, and to support their loved ones before surgery. Out of the corner of my eye, I notice a lone chair in the corner. *See! Being alone does have its benefits*, I think.

Before I can reflect on my misery any longer, I hear my name being called. I hand over to the nurse the few belongings I've packed and accept the plastic bracelet being snapped on my wrist. Within thirty minutes, I'm changed, scrubbed, and lying on a gurney.

Everyone is so cheery here in pre-op. Nurses covered in masks swish in and out through my privacy curtain, introducing themselves, reviewing charts, and making small talk. The IV line is inserted into the top of my hand, and the heart monitors are taped onto different parts of my body.

Reality is setting in, and I'm becoming acutely aware that, in just a few minutes, a laser is going to slice open my neck and remove a part of my body that apparently everyone else needs to survive. How does one live without a thyroid? I want to call a time-out, sit up, and say, "Ya know what? I've changed my mind. Perhaps we can reschedule this for another time."

There's no time left to plan my escape. The anesthesiologist swooshes through the curtain and introduces himself. Standing close to me, he touches my shoulder as he talks directly into my eyes with a mask over his mouth. I'm alert, as I listen to him explain the next steps. I feel the burn of the drugs entering my veins through the IV. My ears are echoing.

"I love my kids," I say out loud, as I drift away.

In the blink of an eye, I'm slowly drifting back to consciousness. I feel so comfortable and warm. I want to stay here forever, but a nurse is gently shaking me, calling my name. I feel her leaning over me, talking in a voice that sounds like it is coming from a distance. "Her breathing is too shallow. Her blood pressure is dropping," the nurse says. She shakes me harder, irritating me. I want to go back to sleep but the shaking continues until I open my eyes. "Breathe. Take a big breath for me," she says sternly. I open my eyes, take a breath, only to feel an intense burning in my throat.

A few hours later, I'm partially awake in my room, waiting for the surgical meds to wear off but hoping they keep the pain meds coming, because I can't feel a thing. Groggy and comfortable in my room, I take in the fabulous view of the city from my bed. My head hurts too much for television, so with the lights dimmed low, I doze off and on.

During one of my hallway walking excursions accompanied by a nurse, we pass a mirror. I catch a glimpse of my incision for the first time, the scar on the front of my neck I'll carry with me forever. The incision is directly between the two clavicular heads located at the base of my neck. I expected stitches and bandages, but find a glued incision covered with a blood-red sterile wax instead. It isn't a dainty wound. I look like a crime victim.

Waking to an emerging dawn outside my window, I watch as the sun reflects off the surrounding buildings, slowly bringing light to another day. I watch as the sun reflects off the surrounding buildings, slowly bringing light to another day. It's a day to live life to the fullest, even if it means I'm stranded in this bed, with my neck held together with wax and glue and my thyroid in a petri dish somewhere in the building.

I lie for hours, watching the different hues of the city as the day progresses. Horns honk outside, and nurses bustle about. Machines beep quietly down the hall. Everyone moves through the routine of their day, except me and the other patients on this floor. Today I'm not a participant. I'm an observer, deep in thought. I'm okay with that.

Later that evening, my surgeon pays me a visit, explaining that his approach in removing the thyroid was correct. Both nodules were malignant. Due to the early diagnosis, my lymph nodes were not affected. Aside from taking a daily dose of Synthroid medication and calcium supplements for the rest of my life, I will not need to do anything further. I am now free of this cancer.

My hospital discharge takes place early the next morning, accomplished with the same minimal fanfare as my arrival. I get dressed, carrying no flowers or well-wishes. Aside from my children, I've told only my mother and my sister. It's just me, with a new story to add to my repertoire of life. It takes only a few steps down the hall of the hospital for me to realize that my incision is more noticeable than I thought. People are staring, trying to look away from the gob of blood-red wax on my neck. I didn't think to bring a scarf.

You never realize how carefree your life has been until you travel through an array of chaotic events. Once again, I'm reminded that I've come so far and I'm still getting through everything that has come my way. I need to be proud of these achievements. At that moment—for no particular reason, lucky to now be on the other side of cancer—I decide the time has come for another substantial change. This transformation will bring me even closer to my unknown destination.

I glide down the escalator and slip through the revolving door, happy to breath in the chilly city air. I hop into Zoey's waiting car. Heading home.

I mentally check another accomplishment off my to-do list. Husband kicked to the curb? *Check.* Filed for divorce? *Check.* Cancer obliterated? *Check.* Good or bad, I'll take whatever comes next.

I am resilient. I am blessed. I've got this.

Chapter 32
The Pool, March 2015

AFTER AVOIDING THE TASK for months, I am finally ready to take on the house damage left behind in Dick's wake and today is a great example of friendship in action. I find myself blessed with help from extended family members, who embrace me with their love and support. In the spirit of family, they arrive to help me complete the numerous unfinished projects and damage that Dick left behind. They clean the basement, unstuff ceilings full of junk, repair drywall, redo the failed bathroom renovation, replace the blown-out air conditioner, and update items throughout the house in an effort to erase Dick's presence.

Winter's fury has left extensive damage, but that's the least of my worries. With most of the heavy snow melted, I have no choice but to now face the most expensive mess of all, the damn pool.

Lifting the plastic pool cover to peek inside, I realize that the sides have collapsed during the winter months. The pool that never was has virtually folded into itself, just as our marriage did. Strangely, laughter is my only response. It's as if the pool just died, gave up, and let me win this battle. I laugh until the chill of the air sends me inside. The saga of this pool has turned out to be a comedy of errors.

Examining the property further, I am not surprised to find that the fence Dick installed just a week before we separated didn't make it through the winter, evident by the chain link blowing loosely in the wind with gaps so wide that the dogs walk under it freely and the deer step over it to graze on the bushes. I chuckle as I walk around the property, looking at shovels and tools scattered on the ground throughout the yard. I laugh because the careless mess reflects my marriage. I am finally going to be free of his clutter, his lies, his intimidation, and his poor workmanship. And I will be rid of this damn pool!

My older brother John, who has always had my back since our childhood, arrives with his backhoe, no questions asked. He rips the pool to shreds, piece by piece. Each snap of the fiberglass being pulled and crushed by the backhoe's claw is music to my ears. A few weeks later, the hole is filled and leveled, the landscapers replace the irrigation system and hydroseed the lawn. I treat the lawn like my special baby, wanting the gorgeous expanse of green grass to be perfect once more. I could not have done it without each person who helped me when I had nowhere else to turn. I am forever grateful for my brother John, my sister Caroline and my extended family who checked in on me and supported me at this difficult time. They took a colossal construction mess and made it right again. Their friendship and good-hearted humor helped me to smile, and I honor each one of them.

Finally, my backyard and my home have been returned to the way they were meant to be.

Chapter 33
April 2015

I LOVE MY HOUSE, but the thought of selling it has been on my mind since I lay in my hospital bed recovering from surgery.

I spend the days that follow gazing into each room, wishing to turn back time to the moments when the home—my dream house—was bustling with the pitter-patter of my three beautiful babies. Running my hands along the smooth surfaces of the walls, I recall how I painted most of them myself. I light fires in all the fireplaces, so I can sit and stare into them, deliberating about what I am about to do. It's my way of saying goodbye.

I raised my children here, creating so many wonderful memories, but something is telling me it is time to change the script of my life's story. I have no definitive plan, no idea where I will go, but I feel a comfort in knowing that things will emerge with each step I take. Sometimes you need to surrender aspects of your life in order to grow. I am ready.

Thinking about moving to a new house in a different state is invigorating. Those who know me worry that I will be running from an abusive husband with the notion that the miles between us will somehow stop him from encroaching on my life. But in the last few months, there's been a shift in my perception that has nothing to do with running away from him. Instead, I have a sense of running toward *me* and the life I would like to see unfold.

I have a history of letting negative thoughts derail me and convince me that my ideas and dreams are unreachable. In my brain, it takes a lot of effort to stay on the positive side, but the dedication to my therapy and my metaphysical teachings has helped me to reach toward better thoughts. I use this training as I contemplate the difficult decision of whether to leave these walls behind me. Can I gather the courage to leave here, newly divorced and completely alone, with my kids exploring elsewhere?

The house that was busting at the seams a few years back, is now too big to wander alone, especially with Zoey leaving for college in a few short months. She's the last of my kids to come bursting through the door each day. I would like to turn evening darkness and months of chilling cold into brighter sunsets and a warmer climate. As much as I love my dream house, I am longing for a new one, a smaller house near the beach, with the sun on my face each morning and the smell of the ocean drifting through the air.

Since my separation, I've slowly been purging eighteen years' worth of accumulated belongings, making way for organized rooms, closets, and drawers. My positive thoughts keep the momentum moving. The time is now.

With the home repairs complete, I move on to the next step. *Why not a private sale?* I think to myself. *I sold my last home on my own. Maybe I'll get lucky twice.* The house is spectacular, and I won't know unless I try. *What's the worst that can happen?*

For the next week, I piece together a three-page sales brochure, complete with glossy pictures capturing the highlights of the home and all the details needed to attract a potential buyer. The listing is posted online, and the brochures will be released to the surrounding neighborhoods. It's such a bittersweet endeavor I am about to undertake.

I have one last dreaded chore before the house goes on the market—tackling the last space that hasn't been cleaned, the garage.

That's the space where Dick hoarded all his junk, the one space I've been avoiding.

He was a hoarder of nails, screws, golf balls, rusted metal, leftover wood, ancient industrial equipment, and every other piece of junk under the sun. The three-car garage is filled to the brim, leaving just one space open for a car to pull in. It's a far cry from the meticulous garage I had prior to his arrival. There's so much clutter that I've ordered a dumpster delivered to my driveway. I find it ironic that the clutter was the first red flag when he moved in, and here it is still, lingering after his departure, waiting for me to pick up his mess.

The dumpster is filled with discarded junk long before I've finished clearing the garage, leaving me no choice but to drag the remaining items to the curb for trash pickup. As the pile grows at curbside, I worry that the trash truck won't take it all. I pile it up anyway, hoping for the best.

All day long, I drag out old blankets, pool equipment, clothes, old engine and motorcycle parts, and an immense cache of half-empty vodka bottles that he kept hidden throughout the garage. And I'd thought I knew all his hiding places.

During one of my trips down the driveway, out of the corner of my eye I see my next-door neighbor at her mailbox. *Shit*, I think to myself, *I look like hell. I have dirt all over my face, my thyroid scar is still healing, my hair is growing out from being chopped off, and my skin hasn't recovered from the trauma of Dick.* I'm not ready to answer any questions, but it's too late now. I've already been seen, and I can't turn back.

I do my best to paint on a smile. "Hi, Alana," I say, sending her a friendly wave as I approach the curb.

Alana is my new neighbor, having moved in next door a year ago. She is recently married, with a blended family of five lively children. She is beautiful and vibrant and always friendly.

"Hey, Stella. How are you?"

"I'm doing okay. Been a long winter." I continue with the small talk, feeling exposed and hoping to avoid any probing questions. "I'm cleaning out the garage, getting ready to put the house on the market. Do you know of anyone who would be interested in buying in our neighborhood? I'm going to sell it myself." I lightheartedly continue with a smile, "Maybe you're interested? Lots more room over here."

She smiles. "It's such a beautiful house. I'm sure the inside is lovely. I'll keep my ears open."

Knowing she has just given birth to their fifth child, I jokingly say, "If you ever want to take a look inside, feel free to give me a call. Fifty-five hundred square feet. Large bedrooms and lots of room to grow."

She laughs at the absurdity of moving again so soon. "We're so busy, but I'll think about it and give you a call." She pauses a moment and then asks, "How's Jake?"

I can feel my nerves spark; my face becomes hot as I answer. "I ended it last November."

"Wow, he's been gone that long? I realized a while back his truck was gone. Are you doing okay?"

"I'm fine. Really. It's much better this way."

She smiles warmly, as we chat a bit longer. We part ways down our parallel driveways—she back to her new marriage and me back to clearing out my old one.

As the afternoon wears on, I get the three-car garage organized in my typical compulsive manner. Its floors have been vacuumed and mopped to a sparkling clean, the cobwebs are gone, and it's ready for showing. I'm freshly showered and relaxing on the couch when my phone rings. It's an unidentified number.

Oh, boy. Do I answer? But my curiosity gets the better of me, as usual. I answer and hear Alana's voice.

"Hi. It's Alana next door. Would you mind if I came over to look at your house? I would love to see the inside. Please don't clean up. I certainly understand what a messy house looks like," she says jokingly.

"Of course," I say. "No problem. How about in fifteen minutes?"

I'm off the couch like a bolt of lightning, running through the house, tidying, and throwing everything into cabinets and under beds.

I vacuum up whatever I can get to and throw the vacuum hose into the basement gym as the doorbell rings. The place doesn't look so bad, given the short notice. Who knew that today I would be opening the door to my first showing and Alana's visit to my home?

My metaphysical studies are coming to fruition: Positive thoughts open so many doors in one's life.

Two of Alana's toddlers run past her to look around the house as she steps into the foyer, scanning the entrance. I watch as she takes in the curve of the grand staircase and the two-story open foyer. Her gaze flows from the French doors to the sunlit rooms with their expansive outdoor views. I continue the tour through the formal living room.

She pauses at the sliding living room door, where I rediscovered myself under the stars, comparing her expansive view of the conservation land to mine. I stand alongside her and realize that the view we share as neighbors is hard to duplicate, this luscious New England beauty. We both have to pull ourselves away from the view to continue the tour.

The hallway has three arched openings that border the dining room, leading to the grandest entrance of all, the newly renovated kitchen. As we enter the kitchen, the sun is shining perfectly on the granite. The wood floors gleam, and the Tuscan blue walls and natural stone backsplash complete the ambiance.

The kids run through the rooms exploring, begging to go upstairs to look at the bedrooms. Instead, I lead them downstairs. "Come with me," I tell them. "I'll show you the world's coolest playroom."

The kids bounce down the stairs to find the perfect family space to entertain and contain their friends, complete with a big-screen television, two spare bedrooms, a full bath, wine closet, gym, mudroom, and its own private entrance. Then, of course, there's the spotless, three-car garage which, in a strange way, has made today's showing possible. This is, in every way, a splendid home for a growing family.

"Wow, your home is so beautiful," Alana says, as she lingers through the tour, becoming more interested as she surveys each room of the house.

Two days later, Alana calls again, asking to bring her husband for a tour. The day after that, she calls to ask if she can bring her mother. A few days later, her college friends arrive for a peek.

At this point, Alana is conducting the tours herself. I stay out of the way, so she and her family can wander freely. Then more family members arrive. Aunts, uncles, nephews, and nieces come next. I stopped cleaning and tidying about three visits ago. With each visit, Alana and I get to know each other better. I like her. I enjoy listening to her ideas for the house, and I adore her kids. There is still no formal offer to purchase the house, but neither Alana nor I feel rushed to make it formal. I stay positive and know that everything will work out for the best, one way or another. But deep down, I think we both know what is happening. It is obvious that my house is going to belong to them.

Alana is a successful attorney, with brains and beauty. She is charismatic and funnier than I realized. She and her husband are a couple in love, with a handful of kids, and I am having such fun watching this unfold for us. Soon we are sharing warm dinners and homemade pesto, hand-delivered to my door by her children.

I've saved my old craft supplies, dress-up clothes, and Halloween costumes in a box for her kids to enjoy. I'm falling in love with her two youngest babies and taking visits from her older kids, who tell me silly stories of their life next door. Her children begin ringing the doorbell to ask if they can invite the other neighborhood kids inside for random tours of their soon-to-be bedrooms. I welcome their presence, as I watch the kids run from room to room. It makes me wish I had gotten to know Alana's family long before it was time for me to leave. All those months, I'd avoided Alana for fear of my own exposure and of the neighborhood gossip that was generated by Dick's 911 calls.

Dick is still delaying the divorce proceedings, which could possibly restrict the sale of my home. In an effort to be proactive, my attorney and I head back to court to seek the judge's permission to sell my house, even though Dick never had any share of ownership during our short-term marriage. The judge is quick to deny my request, despite my offer to put $200,000 into escrow to allow for divorce negotiations. The delay is exasperating, making Dick openly jubilant about the fact that he is keeping me from moving on with my life, even after he had taken the liberty to pursue a scandalous double life throughout the entirety of our marriage. The court's decision has empowered him again. He has now attached himself to the $200,000 figure we offered as being the minimum amount of money he will acquire in our divorce. He was quite pleased when he left court on that day, while I was once more struck down in the eyes of the law.

I know Dick assumes this delay will be a detriment to me, forcing me to lose a buyer, but it just makes me more determined to sell. The judge might have delayed the move-in date, but I won't lose my buyer, as Dick is hoping. Nor does Dick know who the buyer is. He thinks it is a stranger who will move on to a different house if the sale is delayed. He is wrong.

Alana and I continue the old-fashioned way, with a verbal agreement and a handshake. We let things proceed at their own pace, waiting to settle on the house until after the divorce. She wants the house, and I want her as my buyer.

I watch as she decorates my home to her liking. The walls take on new paint colors and the upstairs bedrooms are transformed to suit young children. The girls' bedroom closets brim once more with dolls and stuffed animals. The shower curtains are childlike and bright.

Some might think this process would be a difficult one, having a front-row seat to your own house being transformed by the family who will soon live here, but it works for me. The hardest part turns out to be observing the transformation of my children's bedrooms. It is where they slept, did their homework, and grew up. However, to move forward, I push my emotions aside and realize that many of the rooms of this house have sat empty for too long. I find peace in knowing that Alana's children will have their own giggles and growth in the same space where my children grew up.

Strangely, I need to know the house is in good hands. My intuition tells me that this family is the perfect fit. Alana is making the house young again, and I like it. And while she redecorates, I set my sights on a new home in Florida. A house near the ocean awaits my arrival.

Preparing for the last lap of divorce, we expedite the inspections needed to finalize the sale of the Larington house. That is, until I receive a call from the Larington fire chief, informing me that the house has failed the recent fire inspection.

"How could it possibly fail?" I ask.

My heart sinks as he explains. "Every fire alarm wire in the house has been disconnected and all the wires pulled out. When the inspector removed the main control panel by the front door, he found the circuit board had also been removed, making it impossible to notify the fire/police in an emergency. In Larington, you are required to have hardwired alarms. I don't know how this happened, because you passed inspection when you purchased the home eighteen years ago."

The thought that my children and I were living in a house without fire alarms shakes me to the core. I have no proof of Dick's involvement, of course, but I know of no other person evil enough to do such a thing to a woman and her children. Stripping away our safety is the nastiest form of abuse I can imagine. For me, the true horror is thinking back to his threats to burn down the house, knowing now that, if I had let him stay longer or had not been vocal about the abuse after our separation, he might have acted on his threat.

News of the inspection failure shakes me terribly. Every time I become confident or get a few extra steps away from the layers of his chaos, he finds a way to strike again. Dick has managed yet another delay in the sale of my house. He has again shown me how dangerous he was during our marriage.

Once my divorce is finalized, the transition becomes a reality. Alana and I had a few setbacks, but in the end, I wouldn't have wanted to go through the process with anyone else. For a moment in time, I became part of a happy young family who are elated about their move next door. Their happiness has made it easier for me to leave my dream home behind, as I set out to chart new waters. What fun to have been part of it all!

Who could have known my dream home would sell to a woman I had almost turned away from in shame? I made a friend in Alana at a time when I thought my damage was so transparent and toxic that no one could possibly want to be near me. Alana proved me wrong, thanks to her friendship, her trust, and her refreshing sense of humor.

There was no need to distribute the glossy sale brochures. I reached the goal of selling my home on my own, to a family I handpicked, while going through a brutal divorce from a man who refused to graciously release me, all the while recovering from cancer. It is a stellar outcome, if I do say so myself, just for walking to the end of my driveway, beyond my comfort level, and saying hello.

Chapter 34
August 2015

IT'S BEEN NINE MONTHS since I left my marriage on a cold, November night. My day of reckoning has finally arrived. Today a court judge will hand me back my life, after numerous delays, freeing me from this man. Whatever the outcome, I so badly want it to end that I'll take any decision handed to me, so long as I am set free.

To date, the legal proceedings throughout our divorce have not worked in my favor. It took many weeks and a manhunt to serve him with divorce papers. The court allowed every extension he requested, adding months to the stalemate. I had succeeded in obtaining a restraining order but failed to make the court recognize his violations, empowering him to harass me even more. What little I negotiated regarding a financial settlement, he would accept, only to later rescind, claiming he'd changed his mind and wanted something more. I'd been unable to convince a judge to let me sell my home, despite my offer to place a large sum of money into escrow for the sake of negotiations.

My estranged husband is a man of no morals, and today I go face to face with him. I'm taking a leap of faith out of desperation, leaving the decision in the hands of a judge who knows nothing about me, yet now holds my financial future in his hands. He will speed-read my attorney's carefully written legal brief, size me up, and then allow approximately fifteen minutes of his time to hear both sides, as a roomful of other divorcing couples watch and wait for their turn before the judge. He's on a tight schedule. The odds are not in my favor.

Itching to be free, my mind wanders as I wait for my turn in front of the judge. I have grown to be "far more" than the disgusting words that Dick laid at my feet each day. I've done the work to find my clarity and strength. It is my responsibility to rise from this and build a better life for myself, far away from him. I am here today, to do just that.

Today I am prepared to fight back hard. I know that if Dick is going to go down, he will try to take me with him. *Not this time*, I decide. Today he goes down alone. Under no circumstances will I fail.

My mind snaps back into the moment, as I hear the announcement, "All rise!" The judge enters, and I pray one last time. "Please, God, don't let me be first. I don't want this full house to partake in the embarrassing story of my marriage. I need a moment to sit here, to silently pray for this day and the outcome of what is to be." Looking down at a stack of papers, the judge calls out his first case of the day, "Jacobs vs. Slick."

"Come on, God! It was such a small request!" Exasperated, I rise with my attorney, as do Dick and his attorney. We make our way to dueling podiums to be sworn in for the record. Right hand raised, I nod in agreement to tell the truth, the whole truth, and nothing but the truth, so help me God.

At the end of our allotted fifteen minutes, Dick is awarded a divorce settlement of only $7,500—with his attorney asking the court to order the check be written out to him, because Dick doesn't have the financial wherewithal to pay his own counsel. The most gratifying piece to this happy ending comes when we are sent outside the courtroom to finalize the judge's orders with our attorneys.

Dick proceeds to have a tantrum, while his annoyed attorney begs us to finalize and initial the divorce declaration and write the check immediately, so he will never have to see or talk to this client again. I take pure sadistic pleasure in watching it unfold.

After hearing my case, a few onlookers who were in the courtroom during the proceedings commend me in the hallway, just as others had done after the restraining order hearing months earlier. Strangers tap me on the shoulder and shake my hand to wish me well.

In the end, after this long, torturous expedition, it has taken only fifteen minutes to convince a judge and an entire courtroom of onlookers why Dick had earned the name Dick. I, Stella Jacobs, walk out of court a free woman.

The gates of freedom have finally opened, allowing me to start anew. With an extended restraining order in hand, my heart sings on the day of my divorce, not just because I am no longer his wife but because I can now move away from him emotionally and geographically, to live freely without his ridicule and intimidation. It creates a celebration in my heart like no other.

A few months later, the selling of my home becomes a reality, followed by a long-distance move I have been waiting to execute.

People hesitate when they hear I'm moving out of state, questioning my intentions and asking if I'm in the right place to make such a decision. I've never been more prepared. A few people offer to join me for my freedom ride to my new home. Well-intentioned friends think it is too far for me to drive alone, but I don't want anyone tagging along. I want to do this solo. It's just the three amigos for this road trip.

I'm not running from anything. My strength comes from the adjustments I've made for myself and the things I've learned these past months. I am far stronger than I've given myself credit for and much wiser from the experience. I accept my mistakes, and I take responsibility for my part in the creation of the marriage. After all, conflict between two cannot exist without participation from each party.

I'm quietly transformed and eager to go further in my philosophical studies. My teachings, my goals, and my gratitude are my focal points now. I strive for deeper understanding each day. I don't immerse myself in negative thought, and I avoid pessimistic people, those who always insist the sky is falling.

Believe me, these past few years I've stood directly under a falling sky in the middle of a lightning storm, and I've lived to tell about it. I can't say I came out of it unscathed, but I do appreciate everything I learned from the storm. It might sound trite to the naysayers, but once you learn to live with a consistent vibration of happiness and level of inner peace, you'll be reluctant to turn back. Just walking out of the courtroom with a divorce brought me a sense of peace that I want to carry into everything I do moving forward. My kids, my dogs, and the future ahead are my only priorities.

Preparing for my move, I realized that I no longer wanted to be defined by my belongings, which enticed me to give away most of my possessions, releasing me of a burden I didn't know I had until the clutter was gone. The shift in my thinking left space for me to feel more gratitude for the items and memories that were important enough for me to hold on to.

That's not to say I don't desire nice things, prosperity, and achieving my dreams. I've never been more excited to go after whatever it is I now choose. My aspirations are front and center, and I'm now immersed and focused enough to pursue them with a vengeance. My soul is eager to live in a new place with a blank canvas, mine to paint any way I wish.

I understand why others question my decisions. While I did not recognize the warning signs, and my boundaries were blurred, I was able to recognize the exact moment I needed to jump ship. And jump I did.

The night of November 14, 2014, when he stumbled inebriated into the kitchen with his wedding ring in his pocket instead of on his finger, was when I took the first step of bringing myself back to life.

Since then, I fought for survival to avoid becoming stagnant in thought or action. I battled my abuser every inch of the way and didn't stop, even when I lost many of the battles. I had a strong premonition that I would eventually win the war and finally distance myself from him. While not always evident on the forefront of this journey, I knew deep down that I have always been a brave survivor.

I'm not looking for validation. I'm not looking for sympathy or accolades because I came out on the other end reclaiming my value and my dignity. I was looking for myself. And I found her.

So, here I am. . . . I am the sway of my hips as I walk and a firm backbone that stands taller than before. I am a promising gaze toward the sky rather than dark eyes cast to the ground. I am the sparkle in my smile and the newly acquired inspiration in my soul. I am slightly disheveled from the journey thus far, but tousled in a perfect sort of way. The scars I carry inside and out tell a story. A story of the whole me. The good, the flawed, and the enlightened. So, here I am, far more than I ever imagined I could be, living peacefully and with purpose in a little home near the ocean. Far, far away from chapter one.

Epilogue

AFTER A PILGRIMAGE OF enormous effort, the dogs and I have arrived safely in Naples. Yet the journey has been anything but graceful, despite the poetic poise of our arrival. It's not that I traveled from point A to point B, and now I have some prize in my hand to wave to the crowd. There is no prize and there is no finish line in the evolution of one's self. That's the best part of it all!

With a knowing smile, I wake every day appreciating my place in this world. The healthy emotional space I now live in wasn't a loud victory. It was a quiet awakening with an audience of one. Me.

If I can be a ray of light for just one person who might see something of herself or himself in my story, then my time has been well spent.

Safe travels. Namaste.
With much love,
Stella,
Riley and Bella

Miles Away

My writing is complete,
Leaving my soul exposed.
My despair transposed to relief,
So much stronger than I imagined myself to be.

As I lived it,
I saw myself as weak,
Unworthy for attracting contempt.
Yet here I stand in the aftermath,
With sunshine pumping through my veins,
And clarity shining in my soul.

It took words on the page to prove it to myself.
Some of it unclear until the last word was written.
I am free to go now.
Wherever I choose to wander.
Bruised, but never broken,

Strong and wise from the journey.
I am free from the chaos.

~ Stella Jacobs

About the Book

STELLA JACOBS' FIRST LITERARY composition is influential in changing the perception of overcoming domestic abuse. Told in real time, her story takes you behind the closed doors of trust, confusion and control, exposing how a toxic drip batters the mind and body.

Secretly, Stella decides to rise above her own diminished situation, living with purpose and gratitude: strengthening her voice by tearing down the walls of shame that held her captive. Join Stella as she navigates the twists and turns of love and despair in search of a thousand blessings for never turning back.

There comes a time in one's life when you have to turn away from those who make you feel "less than," so you can move forward to accept the fullness of who you really are. Who you have been all along, but have been unable to recognize.

Jacobs' writing is raw with emotion and a humbling self-reflection of her passage into the light. *Hollow Ground* is a powerful vibration of the soul that will entice readers to approach healing and personal growth in ways they never thought possible.

CPSIA information can be obtained
at www.ICGtesting.com
Printed in the USA
LVHW08*0344060918
589325LV00006B/79/P

9 781504 397742